EAT COOK HONG KONG

ASIA
2000

I'd like to thank Susan Sams, associate editor of the
Post Magazine, South China Morning Post, who conceived
the idea of a weekly food column and encouraged me
to share my food findings with all on a Sunday morning.

Recipes copyright © 2000 Nell Nelson,
except for recipes as attributed.
Photos copyright © 2000 A. Chester Ong
Illustrations copyright © 2000 Rachel Brebner
All rights reserved

ISBN: 962-7160-98-9

Published by Asia 2000 Ltd.
Fifth Floor, 31 A Wyndham Street
Central, Hong Kong

http://www.asia2000.com.hk

Edited by Vicki Rothrock
Designed by Robert Stone
Typeset with Aldus Pagemaker in Matisse and Comic
Printed in Hong Kong by Regal Printing Ltd.

First Printing December 2000

EAT COOK HONG KONG

BY

NELL NELSON

ASIA 2000

To my parents, Jean and Dougal,
who gave me and my brother three
of the best ingredients in life:
love, laughter and the joy of eating.

CONTENTS

INTRODUCTION

Charles II's last words were: "Let not poor Nellie starve."

I, Nell, have taken these words to heart - and stomach - and dream, eat and write about food in my food diary. It's like a secret code. I can remember incidents and people by what I eat. If someone sneakily read an entry in my food diary, they would never guess what happened on a particular day - or night.

Several years ago, a friend told a BBC producer, who was making a programme on people with obsessive habits, about my food diary. The producer, much to my indignation, rang to ask if he could feature me and my food journal. I refused. But several hundred hot dinners later, I agreed to publicise an account of my life as a food writer living and eating in Hong Kong in the Sunday Morning Post Magazine.

The column in the Sunday Morning Post magazine is my 'food diary,' which highlights the best of what I eat every week - from fish ball noodles with homemade chilli paste to the richest, most decadent chocolate cheesecake this side of the South China Sea. Along the way, I picked up the recipes and found out where the best places are to buy Indian spices in Hong Kong or and where you can learn to cook Asian food. I love travelling and have stuck my nose into the world's cooking pots - kimchee in Korea, ginger chicken in Laos, fresh spring rolls from Vietnam and strawberry and cream cheese muffins from New Zealand.

The book is called *Eat Cook Hong Kong*, because that is what I did. I ate first, then asked for the recipes of the dishes I really liked and cooked them at home for my food column. The 60-plus recipes fall into 6 sections: 'Eat Cook Chinese' for easy authentic dishes using local ingredients, 'Eat Cook Comfort Food' for those days when you want to indulge, 'Eat Cook Show Off' for when you crave adulation at the dinner table, 'Eat Cook Feel Good' for when you want to feel healthy, 'Eat Cook Wanderlust' for when you yearn to travel and resources only permit committing the local ferry time-table to heart and 'Eat Cook Drink' for alternatives to the more obvious liquid refreshments.

All the recipes featured in *Eat Cook Hong Kong* can be easily made in Hong Kong. You can buy most of the ingredients quite cheaply. Don't be frightened of using the local wet markets; they are an integral part of Hong Kong. You don't need a large kitchen - one ring and a toaster oven will do. I know   because I did it. Most of the dishes will feed 4-plus people, but please err on the generous side when cooking, as

4

my greatest fear in life is that there won't be enough. So be sure to double quantities rather than halve them. Relax when you cook and learn to throw a bit of this and pinch of that. And most importantly: Taste as you go along, and you will learn to make dishes you like, not what I like. You only have to be strict about measuring when it comes to baking, so call in the scales for the cakes and muffins.

Eat Cook Hong Kong covers the whole gamut of eating. It includes where to find cooking schools, the best places for sourcing ingredients and an eclectic list of interesting restaurants and private caterers who will do the cooking for you.

Hong Kong is a wonderful stir-fry of cuisines, cultures and people from all over the world. You can eat freshly-spun noodles at breakfast, croissants for elevenses, newly-rolled sushi at lunch, piping hot scones and rose-petal jam for tea, fragrant Thai curry for supper, congee at midnight and a street stir-fry at 3 in the morning.

I hope *Eat Cook Hong Kong* will inspire you to do just that: Cook, Eat and Live Hong Kong.

NELL NELSON

EAT COOK CHINESE

Living in Hong Kong, it is easy to get lazy with cooking Chinese food, as freshly cooked Chinese dishes are sold literally on your doorstep. It is oten easier to go to a local restaurant, especially for a good, noisy morning dim sum session. The street markets are the most fun to shop for ingredients and are a source of some of the cheapest, freshest produce, but you need to start early because things like bean sprouts get snapped up. Desserts are not a big part of Chinese dining; a meal is usually ended with fresh fruit or a sweet bean or nut soup. The dishes here are my favourites, but they represent only a tiny aspect of Cantonese and other Chinese provinces' cuisines.

I went to a four-week dim sum evening class run by the YWCA. Our instructor, Cinderella, demonstrated a dish, then we tried to copy it. The ingredients were all weighed beforehand and we were allocated a gas ring and our own wok, chopper and mixing bowls. Dim sum roughly translates as 'light touches from the heart.' The dim sum classes were on Friday nights; life is definitely too short to spend time stuffing too many wontons, so my dim sum tended to err on the large side, prompting all my Chinese classmates to say that if I ever opened a restaurant it would go out of business. The most successful and easiest dim sum I made was the steamed barbecued pork buns.

Cha Siu Bau Steamed Pork Dumplings

Filling:
175 g roast, skinned pork
(buy from a cha siu shop)
1 tbsp oil
2 shallots, peeled & chopped
2 tbsps cornflour
100 ml water
40 g sugar
1 tbsp oyster sauce
1 tbsp light soy sauce
1 tbsp dark soy sauce

Bun:
200 g plain flour
2 1/2 tsps baking powder
50 g sugar
5-6 tbsps water
1 tsp vinegar
2 tsps lard

For the filling:
Dice the roast pork; fry the shallots in oil. Mix the cornflour with a little water in a cup, till dissolved. Add rest of ingredients and rest of water, add to shallot pan, add pork and cook until sauce thickens and turns glossy and gloopy.

For the bun:
Sift flour and baking powder, add the sugar, then rub in the lard and mix in the water and vinegar, kneading into a pliable lump. Allow to sit for 10 to 20 minutes, then divide into about 8 portions. Fashion – the best word for it – into a circle big enough to accommodate the filling. Fold at the top. Place each bun on a small piece of grease-proof paper. Have a bamboo steamer ready over a wok filled with boiling water. Steam for 10 to 12 minutes – they will fluff up like magic.

Ha Gau Prawn Dumplings

These are one of the more popular Chinese dim sum dishes in restaurants. Remember it takes years for a dim sum chef to be proficient – so don't be disheartened if your dumplings don't merit giving up your day job.

300 g raw shrimp
salt and pepper
75 g cornflour
75 g rice flour
300 ml water

Roughly chop the shrimp and season with salt and pepper. Mix cornflour and rice flour together. Boil water, add the flour and starch mixture, beat quickly with a chopstick to make the dough consistent. Allow to cool. Roll dough into a long, thin sausage, cut off a small piece and flatten with the side of a metal cleaver. Hold the thin dough circle in the palm of your left hand, place a teaspoon of seasoned shrimp in the centre. With the right hand crimp half of the circle together, using your fingertips to make a crescent pocket.

Have a bamboo steamer ready over a wok filled with boiling water. You can line the steamer with lettuce leaves or thin discs of raw carrot to prevent the dough from sticking. Steam the dumplings for 5 minutes.

Perfect Rice

The Cantonese for food is *sik fan* – which literally means eat rice. Rice is an essential part of any Chinese meal and is served usually towards the end of the meal to make sure everyone is full and valuable meat and fish room is not taken up with filling bowls of rice. From street dai pai dongs to five-star hotel kitchens the rice cooker is king of the kitchen. As the rice is steamed, a comforting smell is given off which will always remind me of mealtimes in Hong Kong. The rice is basically cooked in water in a sealed container over an electrical heating element, which effectively steams the rice, banishing the days of stuck, burnt-to-the-bottom-of-the-pan rice forever. The best place to search out a rice cooker is the CRC Department Stores of which there are several in Hong Kong. Such is the Hong Kong passion for rice, there is a whole section on the fifth floor of the CRC in Central devoted to rice cookers. Even with a Deluxe Rice Cooker, there is a science to making rice.

For perfect rice you should rinse the rice in a colander until the water runs clear, but don't be too rough, as the rice grains can chip and cause the starch to escape, resulting in burnt or sticky rice. Add measured rice into the rice cooker and add water to the mark on the non-stick container. A rule of thumb literally - the water should be a half thumb height above the rice. Then let the washed rice soak for 30 minutes, as rice that has absorbed plenty of water will be whiter and more opaque. Lower the lid, plug in and cook (2 cups of rice takes 20 minutes). Be careful not to overcook, as basic models do not have timers. Switch the cooker to warm and let the rice sit for 15 minutes before serving.

Marinated Tofu

From a tin shelter outside my house, an old lady sells trays of fresh, creamy, silken squares of tofu; piles of bean sprouts and soya beans. Tofu is made from cooked, pureed soya beans, which are drained to produce a milky liquid. The liquid is mixed with a coagulant to form soft blocks. The versatile soya bean is known as the 'cow of Asia' as soya bean products are a rich source of proteins, carbohydrates, fibre, fat vitamins and minerals. Soy sauce, which is made from fermented soya beans, wheat, yeast and salt is a staple ingredient in many Asian dishes. Soya milk, which is readily available in Hong Kong, is just ground soya beans mixed with water and sometimes sugar. Chinese department stores sell machines for you to make your own soya milk.

2 blocks of soft tofu

Marinade:
1 tbsp fresh grated ginger root
2 tbsps dry sherry, sake or Chinese rice wine
60 ml soy sauce
60 ml water
1 tbsp dark sesame oil
1 tbsp rice, white or cider vinegar

Optional ingredients:
2 tbsps minced green onions
1/2 tsp sugar or honey
1/2 tsp Chinese hot chilli oil or Szechuan
hot-bean paste
pinch of cayenne pepper
1 tsp toasted sesame seeds

Cut tofu into 2.5 cm cubes. Whisk together all the marinade ingredients and add any of the optional ingredients that appeal to you. Pour the marinade over the tofu cubes in a large bowl and toss gently with a spatula. Chill at least 20 minutes before serving.

Peking Duck

The American Peking Restaurant, fondly referred to as the American Peking, is a stalwart of Hong Kong group dining. Yet, there is not a hamburger or milkshake in sight. More than 50 years ago, the owners, who came from Shandong Province, took over a restaurant in Wan Chai called the American Café. They served Peking food, which is a rich, slightly spicy, oily, noodle/ bread-based cuisine. Then after thirty years, they moved to their current address at 20 Lockart Road. Josephine Chung and her husband Tenny Hou returned from England to take over her father's (one of the original partners) restaurant. The recipes have changed very little in 50 years. In China, Peking duck has always been the special food of banquets. The proper way to eat Peking duck is to place slices of crispy skin, spring onions and a drop of plum sauce on a thin pancake, and then roll it into a pocket. Traditionally, only the skin of the duck was served with the pancakes. The meat was taken back into the kitchen to be cooked with bean sprouts at an additional charge to the customer. The bone of the duck was made into duck soup, which was also served at an additional charge. This was known as 'the duck three ways.'

Recipe for your interest:
1 whole duck fed on a special high-carbohydrate diet
1 hand pump
honey
vinegar
hot water

Clean the duck, then insert the nozzle of the pump in between the skin and flesh of the duck and pump so that it puffs up. This allows the meat to cook evenly and the juices to flow throughout the bird. Marinate, then baste the duck in a honey and vinegar water mix and leave to dry for 3 to 4 hours. This makes the skin crispy. Roast the duck in a barrel-shaped oven over a low charcoal fire for 40 minutes. The charcoal adds a distinct flavour to the birds. Serve with thin pancakes, plum sauce, strips of cucumber and spring onions. Or alternatively, buy a whole Peking Duck plus pancakes, sauce and onions for about $300 to take-away from the American Restaurant, or just eat in.

Szechuan Stir-fried Shredded Beef

I love the sweetness the carrot gives to the beef and also love stuffing the crispy shreds into warm sesame pockets. When we were doing the food shoot, as an incredible treat, I was allowed into the American Peking kitchen to see the pockets being made. The chef expertly poured hot oil onto a mound of flour, kneaded it into a dough, then rolled it out and added more hot oil (layering oil onto dough gives a flaky texture). He shaped it again, then made little balls that he flattened and dusted with sesame seeds. Then he baked the dough till it was golden brown. You could try at home, but for $9 a pocket, life seems too short to struggle with sesame pockets.

400 g sirloin beef

Marinade:
2 tbsps dry sherry
2 tbsps soy sauce
1 tsp sugar
1 tsp cornstarch

Sauce ingredients:
2 tbsps rice vinegar
1 tbsp soy sauce
2 tsps sesame oil
1 tsp sugar
1/2 tsp chilli oil
1/2 tsp cornflour

300 g grated carrot
sliced garlic
honey

Trim and discard fat from beef. Cut beef across the grain into 7.5 cm matchstick pieces. Combine marinade ingredients in a medium-size bowl. Add beef and stir to coat. Set aside for 30 minutes.

Combine sauce ingredients in a small bowl and set aside.

Heat oil in wok, add half of the beef and deep fry for 1 minute until brown, turning occasionally. Lift out and drain on paper towels; set aside. Deep fry remaining beef.

Remove all but 2 tbsps oil from wok. Reheat oil over high heat until hot. Add carrot and sliced garlic; cook, stirring constantly, for 1 minute. Stir in prepared sauce and cooked beef. Cook until the carrot sizzles into corkscrew shapes and the meat turns a dark brown and separates from the fat. Drizzle with honey to make it shiny and serve with sesame pockets or warm pitta bread pockets or even rice.

Four Season Beans

These spicy, green beans are known as four season beans – simply as they are available all the year round.

1 tbsp preserved vegetable
– buy in relish department
of most Hong Kong super-
markets
750 ml peanut oil for deep
frying
500 g string beans,
snapped in half
1 tbsp minced ginger
1 tbsp finely chopped
garlic
100 g ground pork
1 tsp shrimp paste
1 green onion, minced
1 tsp sugar
white pepper
2 tsps dark soy sauce
2 tbsps chicken stock
a swirl of sesame oil

Rinse the preserved vegetables with cold water to wash off the brine and salt; chop. Add the oil to a hot wok and deep fry the beans in 2 or 3 batches for 2 to 3 minutes. Remove all but 1 tablespoon of the oil from the wok. Reheat the wok over high heat. Add the ginger and garlic; stir-fry for 15 seconds. Add the pork and shrimp paste; stir-fry for 1 minute longer. Break up the clumps of pork so that it looks crumbled. Add the green onions, sugar, white pepper and soy sauce; toss together to blend.

Add the rinsed preserved vegetables, chicken stock and sesame oil to the wok. Toss vigorously over high heat until all liquids are reduced and absorbed; it will take about 2 to 3 minutes.

Eggplant & Pork Stir-fry

This takes 10 minutes at most and is Chinese 'fast food' at its best. Feel free to experiment with the chilli – adding as little or as much as you prefer. Add tofu and you have the classic *Ma Po Dofu*, which translates to Auntie's chilli tofu, or omit the pork and you have a vegetarian version.

3 Chinese eggplants (smaller and slimmer than its Mediterranean counterpart)
75 g minced pork
1/2 carrot
1/2 green pepper
25 g tinned bamboo shoots
1 tsp chopped chillies
1 tsp fermented hot chilli-bean paste

Chop all the vegetables into very small pieces. Cut the eggplant into 5 cm strips and quickly deep fry in hot oil. Remove from the pan and sauté with the minced pork, bean paste and chopped vegetables for about 3 minutes, then serve with rice.

Deep-Fried Squid

I went on a junk trip where we ended up eating lunch at Ming Kee restaurant on Po Toi Island, which is near Stanley. Ming Kee is perched over the beach and bay and is the first restaurant you come to after disembarking from the pier. As you walk into this open-air restaurant, with tin roofing and fans whirring, there is a sign warning of the slippery floor, indicating where fish have been making their last dashes for freedom. Ming Kee is a standard seafood restaurant with big, round tables and all the usual favourites: prawns fried in garlic, clams, steamed fish, fried rice, gloopy sweet and sour pork; but I absolutely love their deep-fried salt and pepper squid.

Ming Kee gave me some vague cooking instructions, and said there was a secret ingredient with which they wouldn't part. In Hong Kong, you see freshly caught squid spread out on ice in every seafood wet market. Make sure you choose squid that is 10 to 15 cm long, otherwise it will become too tough when cooked. The fishmonger will weigh the squid and remove any debris, so there will be no danger of being squirted with squid ink. Wash again when you get home and pat dry.

clean squid, cut into rings
lots of cornflour
salt and pepper
red and green chilli peppers, cut into thin slices
oil

Toss prepared squid rings in well-seasoned salt and peppered cornflour, shake off excess. Then fry the red and green chilli peppers in hot oil; remove the cooked peppers, then add floury squid. The oil should be very hot, so the squid cooks quickly and turns into a crispy, golden tangled web. Serve the tangled mass with wedges of lemon for the food-programme look, or you can serve it with bought sweet and sour sauce for the authentic Chinese-restaurant look. The only missing ingredient is the fresh sea air.

Minced Quail with Lettuce Leaves

Han Lok Yuen Pigeon restaurant on Lamma is a popular dining spot and is simply referred to as the 'The Pigeon restaurant.' Set high above Power Station Beach, it's worth the climb; red Chinese walls, white plastic furniture and palm trees make an ideal setting for a long lunch. Worth trying is the roast pigeon split in half, served with a wedge of lemon. Some 340 pigeons from the New Territories meet their end here. Another popular dish is the minced quail served with lettuce and plum sauce. You can easily substitute minced chicken.

100 g cashew nuts
100 g bamboo shoots
100 g quail or pigeon meat, chicken is a common substitute
100 g mushrooms
soy sauce
iceberg lettuce
plum sauce

Finely mince top 4 ingredients. Mix equal quantities of each ingredient and shallow fry until golden brown. Add soy sauce to taste. Serve with crisp washed iceberg lettuce leaves and plum sauce. To eat, coat the lettuce leaf with sauce and spoon a generous helping of quail, roll up and eat.

EAT COOK COMFORT FOOD

This is the kind of food you want to make when it's raining, when the phone doesn't ring and you can't face wheeling a trolley round a supermarket searching for elusive ingredients. And you want to eat NOW! There are 5-minute broccoli frittata or savoury pancakes thrown together in the time it takes to melt a piece of brie, fast puddings that you can wallow in, chocolate brownies and muffins eaten straight from the tin. And it's also comforting that this type of food does not require much effort or a dazzling, white show kitchen - all of these dishes can be created with a toaster oven and 1 burner.

Chickpea & Coriander Dip

This is a lovely, fresh, herby variation on the traditional hummus made with chickpeas and sesame seed paste. The cumin gives it an elusive, earthy taste and the coriander gives it a kick.

1 tin of chickpeas
2 cloves of garlic, crushed
1 tsp cumin
125 ml lemon juice
60 ml olive oil
60 ml chopped coriander

You do need a food processor for this. Whiz all the ingredients except the last two, then with the motor running, gradually add the oil and coriander. Drizzle with extra olive oil and serve with Greek dark kalamata olives and toasted pitta bread.

Hot Artichoke Dip

This is blissfully easy to make – the hardest part about this dip is opening the can of artichoke hearts.

2 tins of artichoke hearts
1 small jar of mayonnaise
1 packet of ready-grated Parmesan cheese
1/2 onion, finely chopped

Drain the tins of artichokes. Combine all ingredients in a bowl. After mixing, transfer to a presentable ovenproof dish and bake in a medium hot oven (about 180°C) for about 20 minutes until golden brown and bubbling. Serve with thin crackers.

Spicy Chickpea Pumpkin Soup

The type of pumpkin – round lantern size or long Chinese – will determine whether you are serving up soup or hot pot. The long, Chinese-style pumpkin, which you buy in the markets, has a higher water content than the smiling-lantern style, so the pumpkin flesh breaks down completely and is prime soup material.

1 whole Chinese pumpkin
3 tbsps vegetable oil
1 medium onion, chopped
2 tsps Thai red curry paste
1 tsp ground cumin
1 tsp ground coriander
2 tins coconut milk
250 ml chicken stock
2 tbsps sugar
soy sauce
4 tins chickpeas, drained
fresh coriander

Cut the pumpkin into small pieces, scoop out the seeds, then peel. Fry the onion until soft, add curry paste and cook for 1 minute, then add spices. Turn up the heat and add the pumpkin chunks, then add coconut milk, stock, sugar and soy sauce. Stir and turn down to a gentle boil. Simmer until tender, then add chickpeas. Sprinkle with coriander, then serve.

Heliogabalus Pasta Pesto Soup

This fragrant, filling soup can be prepared ahead of time. At the last moment, add the fresh tomato salad. Don't stint on the basil; if soup lacks flavour at the end you can add a teaspoon of bought pesto.

I made this soup for a progressive dinner party with an Italian theme, inspired by Roman Emperor Heliogabalus who has gone down in the history books as 'one of the most depraved and perverted emperors in Roman history.' However, his extravagances did create one custom that survives to this day: the progressive dinner party. He gave a banquet in which one course was served in the house of each guest, from the Capitoline Hill to Palatine Hill, then Caelian Hill, and one across the Tiber.

For the party, I was in charge of starters. Two taxi loads of friends moved from sipping chilled flagons of vino to my stuffy flat on a sweltering evening to be confronted with hot bean and tomato soup. (The recipe comes from *Viana's La Place's Verdura: Vegetables Italian Style,* which billed it as a summer soup, hence my choice of starter.) In spite of the temperature, it was surprisingly good – smooth starchy beans and fresh basil-laden tomatoes. Despite not having any slaves, the soup was very easy to shop for and prepare. We moved on to lasagne and pasta in seafood sauce at the next casa, and ended the evening with gelato in Stanley.

Soup:
4 tbsps olive oil
30-40 basil leaves, torn into strips
2 garlic cloves
1/2 tsp crushed, dried chilli pepper
400 g tin white beans
2 litres of vegetable/chicken stock
90 g small, dried pasta shapes
salt and pepper
freshly grated Parmesan
toasted bread
olive paste

Tomato salad:
4 ripe tomatoes, diced
1/4 red onion, peeled and finely chopped
1 tbsp olive oil
20 fresh basil leaves, torn into strips

Brie Walnut & Pear Pancakes

It is always useful to have a vegetarian option up your sleeve – or in your store cupboard – if someone comes to dinner and reveals they don't eat meat. These brie, walnut and pear pancakes are very easy to make. Executive Sous Chef Geoffrey Bone of the Grand Hyatt made me these pancakes as an example of a dish that can be produced in minutes and looks good.

Pancakes:
Buy ready-made pancakes, or make your own:
Batter: Mix 3 eggs, 1 pint milk, 1 tbsp melted butter, 200 g flour and a pinch salt together; spoon onto a hot buttered, saucer-sized frying pan and cook until bubbles appear, then flip pancake.
quince paste – can substitute apple jelly.
brie, chopped – or any leftover cheese. Gorgonzola and Camembert would be good.
walnuts, chopped – or macadamia or pecans
ripe pear, cut into slices

Smear pancake with paste or jelly; add brie, walnuts and pieces of pear and roll up. Cook for 20 minutes in a medium hot oven (about 180°C) or blast in the microwave until the cheese is just beginning to ooze. Serve immediately.

Mix all the salad ingredients in a small bowl; season to taste.
For the soup: heat the oil, add basil, garlic and chilli. Rinse and drain the beans. Add the beans and stock; simmer for 15 minutes. Liquidise a cupful of the mixture; return to the pan. Add the pasta to the soup and cook until al dente. Serve with grated Parmesan and rounds of toast smeared with bought olive paste.

Broccoli Frittata

This was a popular order at the now defunct Wyndham Street Deli, now known as Uncle Willie's Deli. You can vary the flavours by adding any extra vegetables or cheeses you have lurking in your fridge.

150 g broccoli
150 g new potatoes
200 g onions
1 tsp olive oil
3 tbsps red wine
1 tsp sugar
6 fresh eggs, beaten
salt
ground black pepper
100 g Parmesan cheese, grated

Blanch the vegetables by dropping sliced potatoes and broccoli florets into boiling water for several minutes, then drain. Slice onion finely and caramelise by frying in olive oil for one minute, then add red wine and sugar; cook until red wine has evaporated. Set aside.

Heat an oven-proof omelette pan and add oil; when the oil gets hot add the caramelised onions, broccoli and new potatoes. Sauté for 30 seconds, add the eggs and salt and pepper to taste. Loosen the sides of the omelette from the pan, then put the pan in the oven at 180° C for 10 to 15 minutes. Remove from oven, flip omelette onto a plate, garnish with Parmesan cheese and serve immediately.

Roquefort Tart with Red Onion Jam

I made this very easy tart served with a red onion jam or marmalade when I rather impetuously invited my friend the chef round for supper. I think we both were surprised how good it was. The recipe comes from a very user-friendly cookbook called *Fusions* by Martin Webb and Richard Whittington (Ebury Press, 1997).

900 g red onions, thinly sliced
150 ml olive oil
2 tsps castor sugar
salt and pepper
225 g bought frozen puff pastry
1 egg
170 g Roquefort cheese or any other strong-flavoured blue cheese
55 g Ma scarpone - rich Italian cream cheese, can substitute normal cream cheese

First make the red onion jam. Cook the onions gently with the oil for 30 minutes in a heavy pan. Turn up the heat and add the sugar to caramelise the mixture. Roll out the pastry to about 5 mm thick and line a 20 cm flan tin. Chill in fridge while making the filling. Preheat the oven to 200° C. Beat the egg and add the cheeses, beat to a stiff paste and spoon into chilled pastry case. Bake for 20 minutes and serve with the red onion jam.

Sweet Potato Pie

I begged Lori Granito, the ebullient owner of the New Orleans-style restaurant The Bayou, for her recipe (which turned out to be her mother's) for this dense, sweet potato pie, which is popular at The Bayou. Sweet potatoes look like normal potatoes, but are a dusky pink colour. Lori says this pie is usually served during holidays in the United States, but as sweet potatoes grow all the year round in Louisiana, it is often on the dining table. Sweet potatoes are easy to get in Hong Kong markets or even ready-cooked from a street vendor.

375 g cooked, mashed sweet potato
250 g sugar
125 g butter
2 eggs, beaten
1/4 tsp cinnamon
1/4 tsp nutmeg
1/8 tsp ginger
1/8 tsp salt
1 tbsp vanilla extract
125 ml milk
135 ml double cream

20 cm baked pastry shell – bought or made

Topping:
60 g of butter
125 g brown sugar
125 g chopped pecans

Mix the potato with the sugar and butter, gradually add the beaten eggs, then the rest of the ingredients. Pour into baked pastry shell and bake for 35 minutes in a medium hot oven (about 180° C). While the pie is cooking, make the topping: melt butter, add sugar and pecans. Pour the topping over the cooked pie and return to the oven and bake for another 25 to 30 minutes.

Chocolate Marble Cheesecake

I have always coveted the recipe for this stick-to your-mouth-richness cheesecake. Andrea Stedman who set up The Continental in Quarry Bay says the secret is good ingredients – don't even think of using margarine.

Crumb crust:
250 g digestive biscuits
125 g butter

Filling:
500 g cream cheese
250 g castor sugar
3 eggs
250 ml sour cream
1 tbsp orange juice
100 g dark chocolate
1 tbsp water

Crumb crust:
Crush biscuits finely, add melted butter; mix well. Press crumb mixture onto base and sides of greased 20 cm spring form pan. Refrigerate while preparing filling.

Filling:
Beat cream cheese until softened; combine with sugar and beat well. Beat in eggs, then sour cream and orange juice. Pour half of cheesecake mixture into prepared crumb crust. Melt chocolate with water in double boiler over simmering water. Swirl half of the chocolate gently through cheesecake mixture in the crust. Top with the remaining cheesecake mixture, then swirl remaining chocolate through the top half of cheesecake. Bake in a moderate oven between 160° and 180° C for 1 hour or until set. The centre will still move slightly when touched. Allow to become completely cold, then place in refrigerator overnight.

Mandarin Oriental Chocolate Brownies

I love these chocolate brownies – dense chocolate gooeyness with chunks of pecan and chocolate – which you can buy at the Mandarin Cake Shop. Make sure you use the best quality chocolate (with a high percentage of cocoa solids, 50 per cent to 70 per cent), such as Valrhona, which is sold in a big block for cooking.

Mid-bite in my brownie, it occurred to me that brownies are everywhere but in America, which seems to be the acknowledged home of the brownie, they have only evolved on the cake scene in the last 100 years. I consulted a cookbook by Fannie Farmer, who was the Delia Smith of 1890s America. She was the first American authority on cookery. Born in Boston in 1857, Farmer was a director of the Boston Cooking School from 1892 to 1902, when she founded Miss Farmer's School of Cookery, Boston. She edited *The Boston Cooking School Cook Book* (1896); 21 editions were published before her death in 1917. In the original 1896 edition, there is a recipe for brownies, but it is the molasses that gives them their name, not chocolate.

150 g unsalted butter
400 g icing sugar
5 g salt
5 g baking powder
4 eggs
110 g plain flour
150 g pecan nuts
380 g dark chocolate, chopped

Preheat oven to 180° C. Lightly grease a 20 cm square tin and sprinkle with 1 tsp of flour; shake off the excess. Beat butter and sugar together. While they are being beaten, sift flour, baking powder and salt. Melt 200 g of dark chocolate in a bowl over hot water. Add eggs to the butter mixture; beat, then add melted chocolate. Toss the pecan nuts and remaining 180 g chopped chocolate chunks in the flour – this stops them from sinking – then fold in rest of flour mix. Spoon mixture into tin and bake for 40 minutes until a toothpick comes out clean. When cool, sprinkle with icing sugar.

Sticky Banana Pudding
with Vanilla Ice Cream & Honeycomb

This light banana sponge pudding soaks up the wonderful rich caramel and cream sauce pools in the plate, well, like a sponge. One spoonful is never enough of this signature dish from Thai Basil Bar Café in Pacific Place. Thai Basil is fitted out in sleek, contemporary dark teak, chrome, spot lights and slatted wood with not a wooden elephant or padded Thai triangular cushion in sight. And while stock Thai favourites such as pad thai and spicy beef salad are on the menu, the food is very much contemporary Thai.

Caramel sauce:
200 g brown sugar
100 g unsalted butter
150 ml cream

Banana pudding:
2 bananas, skin on
120 g butter
120 g sugar
2 eggs
70 g self-raising flour
1/2 tsp baking powder
1/2 tsp vanilla essence

Honey comb:
125 g castor sugar
125 ml water
1/2 tsp bicarbonate of soda

vanilla ice cream

Make caramel sauce first by simmering sugar, butter and cream together to form a thick sauce. Line 4 dariole tins (you can buy these cup-shaped moulds from the Panhandler, Prince's Building) with some of the sauce, reserving the rest for later. For the banana pudding, preheat the oven to 200°C. Roast bananas with their skins on for 10 minutes until soft and mushy. Cream butter, sugar and eggs, add peeled bananas and fold in flour. Pour into caramel sauce-lined tins. Cover each individual tin with foil. Place in a roasting tin with 2-3 cm of hot water, then cover roasting tin with tin foil and 'steam' in oven for 40 minutes.

Make honeycomb by heating the sugar with water. When the sugar is light gold, add the soda, which will foam; stir and pour onto a tray lined with foil. Cool and crush. To serve: invert the pudding onto a plate. Pour over extra caramel and cream, top with a scoop of good vanilla ice-cream and crushed honeycomb. If you can manage to get your hands on Crunchie bars, they would make a good alternative to making honeycomb, which is a sticky, hot operation.

On a scale of deliciousness these rank "I'd marry you on the spot": sweet warm nuggets of strawberries nestling in pockets of molten cream cheese in an ethereally light sponge. The recipe for these muffins was inspired by one of my happiest moments on a cycling trip in New Zealand from Auckland in the west of North Island to Gisborne in the east. We (150 cyclists on the Bike To The Sun organised cycling tour) had cycled about 50 km in the driving rain along the Firth of Thames coast. We stopped to shelter at a café in Coromandel – and joy of joys – they brought out of the oven a tray of hot strawberry cream cheese muffins. The combination of biting into a freshly baked strawberry muffin with a large white bowl of steaming caffe latte by a roaring log fire will be forever logged in my food memory files, along with the croups of cyclists who had discarded their wet cycling clothes to dry in a launderette and were wearing ill-fitting white overalls, jostling for position by the fire tucking into muffins and coffee.

Makes 6 steroid-sized muffins of statuesque proportions, but if less generous with the measuring spoon makes about 10 smaller muffins.

Strawberry & Cream Cheese Muffins

300 g self-raising flour
125 g sugar
1/4 tsp salt
125 g butter
1 egg
125 ml water
275 g strawberries
250 g cream cheese

Fold all the dry ingredients together. Melt butter, then mix with water and egg. Very gently fold the dry ingredients into the mixed liquid using a fork, taking great care not to over mix. Then add finely chopped strawberries and cubed cream cheese. Grease only the base of the muffin tin, not the sides, so the muffin mixture can rise. Spoon into each muffin cavity, filling almost to the top. Bake for about 20 minutes at 200° C until golden brown.

Cranberry and Camembert Muffins

These are delicious straight from the oven - molten camembert and intense sunshine bursts of dried cranberry-scented sponge.

300 g self-raising flour
2 tbsps castor sugar
2 eggs, lightly beaten
1 1/2 tbsp cranberry sauce
75 g dried cranberries
125 g Camembert cheese, roughly chopped
250 ml plain yoghurt
125 ml milk
60 g butter

Grease 12 x 80 ml capacity muffin tins, but only half way so it is not too slippery for the muffin mixture to get a grip as it tries to rise. Sift dry ingredients into a large bowl, stir in eggs, cranberries, sauce, cheese, yoghurt, milk and butter. Fill the tins 3/4 full to give that generous, active-volcano look to your freshly baked muffins.

EAT COOK SHOW OFF

Sometimes cooking for friends should be more than just a sharing of calories. For special occasions, it is nice to show that your skills transcend boiling a kettle and opening a packet of pasta. These recipes will show you care, but also mean you can't just decide an hour before dinner that you care. It will take time to track down some of the ingredients, and some recipes demand overnight treatment. Your forward planning will pay off at the dinner table.

Ingredients:
Parma ham slices,
can of artichokes,
basil leaves,
(big, good quality),
wooden chopsticks broken in half or use lemon grass sticks,
olive oil for coating pan,
pesto sauce

Parma Ham Rolls

I first had these stunning looking appetisers as part of Tott's Asian Grill & Bar lunchtime buffet. Tott's on the 34th floor of the Excelsior Hotel, Causeway Bay, is a great place to drink a cocktail while enjoying views over the harbour.

Wrap a slice of Parma ham round each artichoke, place a leaf of basil on top and spear with a chopstick. Place in an olive-oiled baking dish and bake for about 5 to 10 minutes in a medium hot oven (about 180° C) until the ham is slightly crisp. Serve anointed with pesto sauce. Obviously, Tott's is catering to large numbers, but for smaller-scale dining, you could always substitute sticks of lemon grass, which will impart a glorious smell and subtle flavour.

Tomato & Gin Mousse

Looks can be deceptive – this innocuous-looking white mousse masks an intense tomato flavour. The cream and gin only enhance the experience. This recipe comes from Christof Syre, former executive chef and Bernard Mayer, executive sous chef of the Regent Hong Kong. This dish is served at the Regent's Plume restaurant.

1 kg well-flavoured tomatoes
(should yield about 250 ml juice)
salt
15 g powdered gelatine
lemon juice
150 ml gin
2 tsps champagne vinegar (or leftover champagne)
salt
sugar
cayenne pepper to taste
90 ml whipped double cream
basil leaves for decoration

Dice tomatoes, then blend and add salt to taste. Put the tomato mixture in a muslin bag and hang over a bowl – to catch the juice, which will be clear in colour, not red – in a refrigerator overnight. Following the instructions on the packet, soak gelatine in warm water. Blend tomato juice with lemon juice to taste, then add gin, champagne vinegar and the soaked gelatine, salt, sugar and cayenne pepper to taste. Fill a large bowl with ice and whisk the tomato mixture in a smaller stainless-steel bowl which sits inside the bigger bowl. Gently fold in whipped cream, then spoon into tall wine glasses and garnish with a basil leaf.

Thai Basil Coconut Prawns with Ginger Lime Drizzle

These fat coconut-matted crustaceans, bathed in ginger-lime coating are the ultimate deep-fried prawn. Thai Basil Bar Cafe Chef James Lockett pioneered this method, which plucks the prawns out of restaurant deep-fried mediocrity. Do not even consider substituting desiccated coconut or tinned pineapple for the fresh ingredients when making this at home.

Ingredients:
Beer batter:
3 tbsps self-raising flour
1 tbsp cornflour
1 tbsp ice-cold beer

Ginger Lime Drizzle:
2 fresh ginger roots
2 cups white sugar
8 cups water
juice of 6 limes

Prawns:
3 medium sized prawns
flour seasoned with salt and white pepper
vegetable oil
shredded fresh coconut
fresh pineapple

To make the batter: sift dry ingredients, whisk in beer and leave in fridge. The carbonated alcohol adds froth and air to the batter.

For the drizzle: combine sliced ginger root, sugar and water and bring to the boil, then simmer for an hour until it is a thick syrup; cool, add lime juice, blend, then sieve.

Peel prawns, remove heads and de-vein. Coat in seasoned flour, then dip in beer batter; coat with shredded coconut and deep fry in vegetable oil until golden brown – takes about 2 minutes. Serve on a round of fresh pineapple with a drizzle of sauce.

White-Truffle Risotto

This dish came about when I went to a white-truffle photo shoot at Nicholini's restaurant at the Conrad International Hotel. I have always loved their white-truffle risotto, which is only available in November when these Italian prized fungi come into season. White truffles are infinitely nicer than black – they have a richer more complex flavour and cannot be preserved or canned. I was hoping I might score a few truffles to use for cooking at home that night. "Dream on" said the Conrad in the nicest possible way, as one Piedmont truffle costs HK$3,000 – about HK$120 a gram. But after the photographers departed, with permission, I collected the shavings from the six uneaten dishes, netting a haul that any self-respecting truffle pig would be proud of and added them to a basic risotto. When truffles aren't in season, you can always add a spoonful of truffle-infused oil at the end of cooking.

30 g butter
175 g Arborio rice
750 ml stock
dash of red wine
100 g Parmesan cheese, grated
100 g dried mushrooms
white-truffle shavings or white truffle oil

Soak the dried mushrooms in water until plump (keep the mushroomy water and add it to the risotto with the stock). Melt the butter and add the rice; gradually add the stock until the rice has absorbed all the stock. Then add red wine, cheese and mushrooms. Just before serving, add the white-truffle shavings and as the heat hits the truffle, a most glorious rich smell will fill the kitchen.

Lotus-root chips

The lotus root grows under water in paddy fields and the lotus flower blooms above. You can buy lotus roots easily in the markets – they look like strings of sausages made of potato. Like the ugly duckling, the dull root is transformed into a beautiful swan. When it is cut into slices the lotus becomes a delicate collection of miniature lacey doilies.

1 long lotus root
flour
olive oil
sea salt

Cut lotus root across the way as finely as possible into discs. Soak the discs in water for half an hour, then dip in flour and shallow fry in olive oil. Serve sprinkled with sea salt.

Cumin Mint Lamb with Roasted Corn & Shallot Salad

This is a brilliant combination of flavours and makes a change from the usual lamb and mint sauce duo. Private caterer Liz Seaton often serves this dish for her clients' dinner parties. It is easy and quick to do at the last minute – if you have the salad already prepared.

Salad:
1 packet whole baby corn
8 shallots, peeled & sliced
2 tomatoes, deseeded and sliced
4 chives, snipped
juice from 1 lemon
2 tbsps olive oil
1 tbsp balsamic vinegar

2 lamb loins

Lamb Marinade:
10 fresh mint leaves, shredded
2 tsps cumin seeds
2 tbsps olive oil
1 tbsp balsamic vinegar
1 tbsp white wine
fresh spinach for decoration

Heat a couple of spoonfuls of olive oil in a frying pan. Trim the ends of the baby corn and fry until just lightly golden, but still crunchy. Mix fried baby corn with other salad ingredients and leave in fridge. Mix the lamb marinade ingredients together and marinade for at least 30 minutes. Brown lamb on both sides, then cook in a medium hot oven (about 180° C) with the lamb marinade – 3 minutes for rare, 6 minutes for medium, 10 minutes for well done. Serve the corn salad on a bed of spinach and coat the cooked lamb with marinade poured over the top.

Tuna Salad that will take you places

When Australian Chef Geoffrey Bone came to the Grand Hyatt Hong Kong for a job, he was asked to cook a dish for the interview panel; naturally, he cooked the dish that had won him a gold medal at the 1999 Salon Culinaire – yellowtail tuna with pickled baby carrots, wasabi cream and apple. The Grand Hyatt panel were equally impressed and Bone was offered the position of executive sous chef.

Tuna:
250 g tuna fillet, trimmed
chives, snipped
1 green apple, skin on, diced
60 g green apple cut into strips as a garnish
sea salt and white pepper
5 ml freshly squeezed lime juice
10 ml vegetable oil

Wasabi Mayonnaise:
2 g Dijon mustard
1 egg yolk
10 ml white vinegar
60 ml vegetable oil
10 ml pickle syrup
5 g wasabi powder mixed with water to paste
pinch sea salt and white pepper
few drops lemon juice
10 g horseradish, freshly grated

To make the mayonnaise: beat oil, vinegar and egg yolk together; add rest of ingredients.
For pickled carrot: boil the sugar, water and vinegar together; add the diced carrot and leave to infuse for a few hours.
For tuna: chop the tuna and place in a bowl and add the lime juice, apple, oil, salt, pepper and chives. Toss ingredients together and place in the centre of a plate like a giant ball.
Dress with wasabi dressing and garnish with pickled carrot and sliced apple.

Smoked Haddock & Chive Soufflé

This is the perfect dish to make if you want to show off and impress friends with your cooking prowess. The trick of recooking the soufflé after it's half cooked means you have more control over timing and it always lives up to its name and rises to the occasion. Soufflé comes from the French verb *souffler*, which means to blow or to puff up. A soufflé is basically a sauce to which you add egg yolks, beaten egg whites and a flavouring or purée, such as seafood, fruit or vegetables, then bake until it puffs up. Have fun experimenting with this twice-cooking method. Serves 6.

175 g smoked haddock, chopped
225 ml milk
40 g butter
40 g plain flour
4 large eggs
salt and pepper
1 small bunch chives, snipped
tub of sour cream
sprigs of dill

Melt the butter, add the flour and stir to a smooth glossy paste. Cook for 3 minutes, then add the milk – whisking all the time; season to taste. Remove from the heat and add 4 egg yolks one at a time; add the haddock and chives. Whisk 4 egg whites and fold into the haddock mixture using a metal spoon. Divide the mixture between the buttered ramekin dishes and place the dishes in a baking tin, then pour some boiling water into the tin. Bake for 20 minutes and remove from tin. When cool, remove soufflés from ramekins; they can now be stored for up to 24 hours covered with clingfilm. When you are ready to reheat the soufflés, cook in a medium-hot oven (about 180°C) for 15 minutes. They will puff again; serve with a spoonful of sour cream and a sprig of dill.

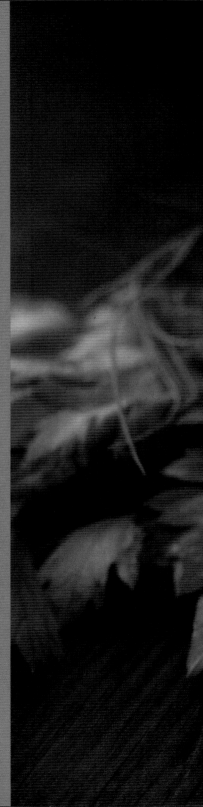

Cappuccino Crème Brulée

This is a gorgeous variation on a familiar theme. As well as looking attractive, it makes logical sense to serve this coffee-flavoured custard in a cup and saucer. The recipe is from Italian restaurant Milano in Wanchai.

1 litre cream
300 ml milk
30 g ground coffee beans
170 g sugar
10 g coffee powder
8 egg yolks
3 whole eggs
70 g sugar
brown sugar
mint sprigs

Heat cream, milk, ground coffee beans and 100 g sugar in a bowl over a pan of hot water. Add the coffee powder and stir until dissolved. Beat all the eggs together with the remaining 70 g sugar and gradually add to the warm milk mixture; cook for a few minutes until thicker. Strain the custard and pour into 8 coffee cups. Place the coffee cups in a baking tin of warm water and bake in medium hot oven (about 180° C) for 45 minutes until the custard is set. Chill, then sprinkle with brown sugar, blast under a hot grill until the sugar melts. You can also buy small, inexpensive blow torches from local plumbing shops to melt the sugar. Serve each cup with a saucer and spoon, biscuit and a sprig of mint.

This pudding tastes infinitely nicer than you can imagine; the pink peppercorns pleasantly jolt the sweet gooey meringue out of its complacency on the pudding rankings. Yet it is not unpleasantly hot, as pink peppercorns are not actually peppercorns – they are the fruit of a plant that grows on Reunion, a French island near Madagascar.

4 egg whites
250 g castor sugar
1 tsp cornflour
1 tsp vinegar
2 tsps pink peppercorns, crushed
1 litre cream (keep chilled, makes it easier to whip)
2 boxes raspberries

Pink-peppercorn Meringue with Raspberries & Cream

I first discovered the spiced-up version of meringue at dinner at my friend the chef's house. Also present at the feast was Lucy Humbert, owner and chef at Lucy's Restaurant in Stanley. So impressed was Lucy by this injection of spice, she substituted the peppercorn pavlova for her normal pavlova on the restaurant menu the next day. Going by its full title of Pink Peppercorn Pavlova, Lucy says nobody ordered pavlova that evening, which was unusual. The next night when customers ordered plain pavlova, the staff dished up the pink-peppercorn-studded number – people ate it without questioning the pink balls of spice.

Preheat oven to 200° C. Using an electric mixer, beat egg whites and a pinch of salt until soft peaks form, then add 3 tbsps sugar and beat for about 3 minutes until sugar dissolves. Add remaining sugar in batches, beating until sugar dissolves. Beat until the mixture is smooth and glossy. Add vanilla and vinegar and beat until combined. Fold in cornflour and peppercorns and spread mixture into 2 even circles on a greased baking paper-lined oven tray. Reduce the oven heat to 120°C and bake meringue for 1 hour, turn oven off and leave the meringue to cool in the oven. Whip the cream and sandwich the cream and raspberries between the meringues.

Cake:
3 washed, unpeeled oranges
6 eggs
250 g ground almonds
250 g castor sugar
1 tsp baking powder

Ice Cream:
350 g castor sugar
250 ml water
8 eggs
250 ml concentrated orange juice (either use bought concentrated orange juice or boil 1 litre of fresh orange juice until reduced to 250ml)
crushed seeds from 10 cardamom pods
600 ml cream

Orange Almond Cake
with Orange & Cardamom Ice cream

Elgin Tastes on Elgin Street belongs to the multi-adjective-menu school of cooking: sun-dried, seared, char-grilled and tossed. The dictionary definition of 'taste' is written across the whole front window – appropriately for a restaurant with such a descriptive menu – which gives an airy feel to the restaurant when inside, without the sense of being in a goldfish bowl. I enjoyed a particularly luscious orange and almond cake served with orange segments and cardamom and orange ice cream. The cake is unusual in that you use no flour and the whole fruit – pith, skin and juice – is used, which is not surprising with such a very vivid, dense orange-flavoured cake. You can vary the citrus tang with a mix of limes and lemons.

Oranges for decoration:
Boil oranges for 2 hours in a saucepan of water. Cool. Slice cross-wise through the centre and remove all seeds. Blend eggs, ground almonds, castor sugar and baking powder with the cooked oranges in a food processor until smooth. Butter and flour a 23 cm tin and bake for an hour at 190° C. Cut oranges for decoration into segments, sprinkle with sugar and keep in fridge until ready.

To make the cardamom and orange ice cream: make a syrup with castor sugar and water. Beat eggs with the warm syrup until the volume is doubled. Add concentrated orange juice to the cooled mixture, then add crushed cardamom seeds and cream. Freeze, beating the mixture several times to prevent ice crystals from forming.

Serve the cake wedges dusted with icing sugar, a scoop of ice cream and orange segments.

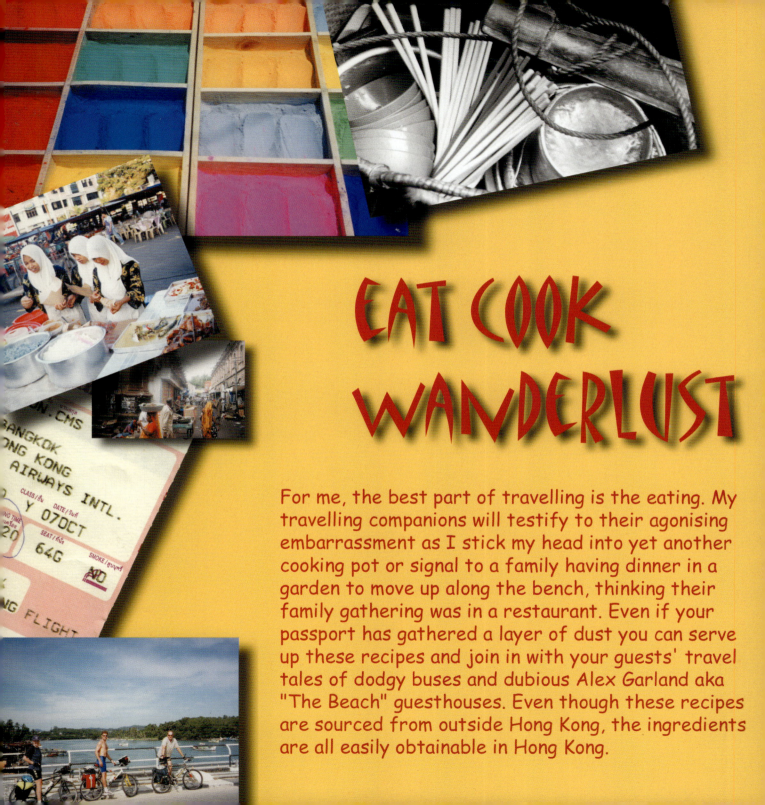

EAT COOK WANDERLUST

For me, the best part of travelling is the eating. My travelling companions will testify to their agonising embarrassment as I stick my head into yet another cooking pot or signal to a family having dinner in a garden to move up along the bench, thinking their family gathering was in a restaurant. Even if your passport has gathered a layer of dust you can serve up these recipes and join in with your guests' travel tales of dodgy buses and dubious Alex Garland aka "The Beach" guesthouses. Even though these recipes are sourced from outside Hong Kong, the ingredients are all easily obtainable in Hong Kong.

California Sushi Rolls

These rolls are not as difficult to make as they look. I went to a sushi cooking class at The Peninsula Hotel and learnt a few tricks of the sushi trade. Senio Sushi Chef Tony Chiu, who made the roll pictured here, can make and roll a California roll in five seconds, which gives him an average speed of 12 spm (sushi per minute). You can buy sheets of dried seaweed, pickled ginger and sushi rice in Sogo and city'super. Sushi rice has glutinous properties, which makes it easier to mould into balls; you can use normal rice, but unless you overcook it, it is less malleable.

sushi rice
sushi vinegar (rice vinegar with syrup and additives)
salt
sugar
dried seaweed sheets
crab sticks
mayonnaise
avocado
orange fish roe
pickled ginger

To make the rice for sushi, wash twice in water to remove some of the starch, then cook in a rice cooker. Mix in by hand some vinegar, salt and sugar to give a slight tangy taste. Leave to cool. Take a strip of seaweed and break it lengthways so it measures approximately 25 cm x 10 cm. Prepare a bowl of iced water, dip your hands in the water so they are moist and cold, but not dripping; take a palm-sized handful of the rice and lay it diagonally from lower left to upper right across the left-half end of the seaweed. Holding one end of crab stick, beat the other end to release the fibres, then lay at right angles across the bed of rice; add a dollop of mayonnaise, a few strips of finely sliced avocado, then take the bottom left corner and fold it toward the top, to form a right angle. Bring the top right corner down to make a cone. Anchor the spare corner with a grain of rice. Top with bright orange fish roe and serve with some pickled ginger.

Mrs Choi's Kimchee

After four days of foraging and feasting in Korea, it was with some nervousness that I checked in my luggage. I took note of the forbidden items to take on board an aircraft: butane gas, camping fuel, matches, explosives, but no sign saying 'no kimchee'. Kimchee is the national dish of Korea and this pungent fermented cabbage is served at every meal and could well have the same properties as those goods banned by airlines. I was carrying a whole fermenting cabbage from Mrs Nan Hwa Choi. Choi is the head chef of the prestigious Korean restaurant Sorabol at The Shilla Hotel, Seoul. For more than 20 years she has been supervising kimchee making and she gave me a lesson and a kimchee (hotel guests can buy one for HK$200). This is the kimchee pictured here, which was flown back on Korean Air at considerable risk to myself and other passengers.

I learned during a tour of the Korean Air Catering Center that Korean Air does not serve kimchee on any of its international flights because of its pungency, another reason why I was hesitant about the repercussions of carrying kimchee aboard. In the old days, kimchee would be kept in large stone jars, which you still see outside houses in Korea. These jars are more likely to harbour plants, as people in Korea have two fridges – one for the kimchee and one for the rest of their food.

1 long green cabbage (not round)
rock salt
1 salad radish
paprika
fresh anchovies and anchovy oil
olive oil
garlic
sugar
vinegar
1 leek
red pepper
spring onions
pear

Take off outside leaves of cabbage and cut in half longways – making sure leaves are all still attached at base. Add a handful of rock salt to a bowl of cold water, rub salt between cabbage leaves and leave cabbage to soak in water for 12 hours. The cabbage will become shrivelled and limp. Wash again in water. Cut radish into long slivers. In a separate bowl, add paprika, salt and fresh anchovies. Mix the vibrant red concoction with hands; add olive oil, garlic, sugar, vinegar and chopped leek, then spring onions, diced red peppers and a little chopped fresh pear – which will all break down. Smear mixture all over cabbage and between cabbage leaves. Leave cabbage at room temperature for a day to ferment then store in a cold place for up to 2 weeks.

Balinese Barbecued Fish Cooked in a Banana Leaf

Bring these easy to transport banana leaf parcels to a barbecue and you will be guaranteed to be on the BBQ guest list for life. I watched, rolled, then ate these fish parcels at the Ritz-Carlton Bali cooking class. This is the most fragrant fish I have ever tasted, as the banana leaf protects the fish from drying out in the intense heat of the barbecue. Don't be alarmed by the list of ingredients; just make one trip to the Thai grocery shops in Wan Chai (see shopping section at back of book for a good, cheap and fresh source of banana leaves, Thai herbs and spices). The Balinese usually don't eat together, except on special occasions such as birthdays and religious ceremonies. The women in the compound prepare the food in the morning, and members of the family will come during the day to help themselves; there is no area allocated in the compound for eating, so dishes like these banana parcels are very typical of Balinese fast food on the run.

500 g chunky white fish fillets, cut into rectangles; you can also use frozen fish
360 ml thick coconut milk
1 egg
3 kaffir lime leaves, finely sliced
1 tsp salt
sugar to taste
10 pieces of banana leaf measuring 24 cm x 16 cm
toothpicks

Spice Mix
4 Macadamia nuts
8 dried chillies
40 g galangal
10 g turmeric root
2 stalks lemon grass
15 g shrimp paste
10 shallots
1 tsp coriander powder

Throw all of the spice mix ingredients into a blender with the coconut milk, then add 200 g of fish, whiz to a smooth paste. Transfer to a bowl and stir in the lime leaf, egg and seasoning. Hold the banana leaf square over a gas flame to make it pliable. The leaf won't burn as there's so much moisture in it; the leaf will turn a lovely glossy green as the heat transfers through it. Place a spoonful of paste on the leaf, top with a piece of fish fillet, then add some more paste. Roll like a tube, then twist the ends at right angles and secure with a toothpick. Repeat until you have used up all the fish and leaves. Cook over hot charcoal for about 10 minutes. Serve hot or cold with rice or just eat as a snack.

Thai Rice Cakes with Spicy Crunchy Peanut Sauce

This blissfully easy starter was inspired by some rice cakes with peanut and minced pork sauce that I enjoyed in a restaurant in Bangkok – a gorgeous old Thai house that had been converted into a restaurant with a huge mango tree in the courtyard.

30 ml oil
3 garlic cloves, chopped
1 tbsp red curry paste (best to buy in a jar from Oliver's as you won't need a whole sachet)
120 ml coconut milk
250 ml stock
1 tbsp sugar
1 tsp salt
1 tbsp lemon juice
4 tbsps crunchy peanut butter
4 tbsps dried breadcrumbs

Heat the oil; add the chopped garlic and fry until golden brown. Add the curry paste, cook for a few seconds. Add the coconut milk, mix well; cook. Add the stock, sugar, salt and lemon juice. Cook for a few minutes, then add peanut butter and breadcrumbs – the breadcrumbs soak up the liquid so the sauce will thicken. Serve with rice cakes. A packet of about 15 dried rice cakes costs HK$10 from the Thai shops in Wan Chai. The purple-coloured rice cakes you'll see there are made from unpolished long grain rice with a bran coating.

Right-on Travellers' Banana Pancakes

When you see a banana pancake on a menu in Asia, it is a sure sign that you are on the backpacker circuit. Thailand scores very highly on the banana pancake index. Vietnam scores well only in the main cities and in some popular beach towns, while Malaysia and Singapore are both home to the pancake; there are pancake pockets in India and even China – Yangshuo by Guilin the most notable – and not even landlocked Laos is immune to the invasion.

Yet where does the banana pancake come from? In none of these countries – where bananas are plentiful – do the local people eat banana pancakes. Small cafés catering to Westerners in Southeast Asia mainly offer them. But the banana pancake isn't common in cafés or homes in the West, either. If it were a case of homesick travellers, there would be Asian interpretations of Weiner Schnitzel, beans on toast and apple pie in the region's kitchens.

250 g flour
60 g sugar
250 ml milk
2 eggs
3 tsps melted butter
1 tsp vanilla essence
1 tsp salt
3 bananas

To make the batter: sift the flour and sugar; add the milk, eggs, melted butter, vanilla essence and salt. Beat until smooth. Heat a lightly greased frying pan; spoon 3 tbsps of batter onto the pan and it should spread out to the edges. Add sliced banana on top and cook until the edges crinkle up; flip and cook for 1 more minute.

Lao Chicken in Ginger & Coconut Milk

Laos is landlocked by Thailand, Cambodia, Vietnam, China and Burma, and was part of French Indochina until 1941. The moment you cross over the Friendship Bridge from Thailand into Laos you know the French have been here, not just from the buildings clad with shutters, but the food.

Lao dishes are very hot with ginger, mint, coriander, lemongrass and coconut. The book *Traditional Recipes of Laos* inspired me. The 30-year-old recipes are those of royal chef Phia Sing and are very much on the lines of: First catch your chicken/buffalo. Gut it and roast it over an open fire. I adapted one of the recipes to recreate a favourite Lao dish.

    3 sticks of lemon grass
    fresh ginger, chopped
    1 fresh chilli
    4 shallots
    1 tin coconut milk
    cooking oil
    6 chicken thighs with skin still on

Whiz the lemongrass, chopped fresh ginger, chilli, shallots and a good slosh of tinned coconut milk in a blender to make a paste. Fry the paste in several tablespoons of oil – this releases the flavours. Then fry chicken thighs in the cooked paste; add more coconut milk to make a sauce and cook for about 45 minutes until chicken is well cooked. Serve with rice.

Vietnamese Rice-paper Rolls

Vietnam was also colonised by the French and the legacy of baguettes and coffee is still very strong. In Vietnam, the coffee is made in adorable two-tier filters, which take forever to drip through. Herbs are an incredibly important part of the cuisine; there are many different kinds of mint, basil and herbs with no English translation. A popular morning drink is herbs, water and sugar all whizzed together in a blender. Around 4 o'clock in the afternoon everything stops for a spring roll in a Vietnamese village. Impromptu stalls spring up by the kerb and rolls are rolled to order for take away or you can sit on little stools and watch the roller deftly assemble rolls to be eaten on the spot.

12 round 20 cm rice-paper wrappers (available from Oliver's in the noodle section)
85 g rice vermicelli
60 g shredded iceberg lettuce
200 g bean sprouts
1 medium cucumber, peeled, seeded and cut into long, thin strips
1 carrot grated
12 large cooked shrimp, peeled, de-veined and cut in half lengthwise (optional)
12 large sprigs of mint
12 large sprigs of coriander

Soak the rice vermicelli in cold water for 20 minutes. Drain and gently separate with fingers. Drop into boiling salted water and cook for 30 seconds. Drain, then rinse in cold running water. Cut into 6 cm lengths. Mix the lettuce, bean sprouts, cucumber and carrot in a large bowl and toss with fingers. Working with 2 rounds of rice paper wrappers at a time, brush both sides with warm water. Wait for about 2 minutes until they soften. Place a sprig of mint and coriander in a line across the lower third of the wrapper. Top with rice vermicelli, arranging it in a log shape. Then add shrimp, lengthwise. Fold the bottom flap of wrapper up and over the filling, then roll it up gently but tightly, folding the sides as you go. The rice paper will seal by sticking to itself. Serve with a Vietnamese dipping sauce - fish sauce mixed to taste with sugar, fresh lime juice, sugar and vinegar. Makes 12.

Nepalese Daal Bhaat

Nepalese food is similar to Indian with Chinese/Tibetan influences such as steamed or fried vegetable or meat dumplings called momos. The national dish is daal bhaat, boiled rice (bhaat) with a thin lentil sauce (daal), accompanied by curried vegetables (tarkaari) and possibly a dab of pungent pickle (achaar). Daal bhaat is the staple food of Nepal and on a trek to Everest Base Camp, this gently spicy lentil dish was a source of valuable fuel along the way as well as in Camp. Base Camp (5,360m) itself is a collection of about 150 tents put up at random on the glacier. There were 12 teams at Base Camp and each team had built its own lodge for communal eating. The large stone-walled lodge we ate in had a tarpaulin roof and stone banquette seating covered with Tibetan carpets which made it seem amazingly homely. Hanging from the wooden support beam were inflated Bacardi rum bottles (courtesy of one of the climber's sponsors). A gong sounded dinner at 7 pm and I joined about 12 Michelin-man-like people in down-padded clothes who talked with ex-citement about going up 'the hill to-morrow' over tomato soup, daal bhaat, curried vegetables and fresh tomato salad, followed by hot tinned fruit salad.

4 cloves peeled garlic, finely chopped
2-3 tbsps fresh ginger, finely chopped
1 tbsp oil
3/4 tsp turmeric
1/2 tsp cumin
pinch of salt
1/4 tsp ground cardamom
370 g daal, sorted and rinsed
(you can use split peas or lentils as a substitute)
1.5 litres water

In a heavy pot, sauté garlic and ginger in oil for 5 minutes. Add spices and sauté a moment more. Add lentils and water, and bring to a boil. Reduce the heat and simmer uncovered for 1 hour – or until the daal is tender. The final result should be soupy and mild flavoured.

Happy Camping Rice with Apricots, Raisins & Almonds

This dish was discovered through necessity when cycling and camping in western China and we ran out of provisions. Our 'kitchen' consisted of a bag of rice, peppercorns, rock salt, almonds and several sachets of free snacks – dried apricots and raisins, courtesy of Xingiang Airlines. One day, a few locals came to inspect our campsite and brought us a bowl of homemade yoghurt. The resulting dish tasted better than anticipated. Fruit, rice and nut combinations are not new. In the cookbook *Persian Cooking - A Table of Exotic Delights* by Nesta Ramazani, there are many recipes for meat, fruit, yoghurt and rice combinations. We were probably not the first to enjoy such a dish as we travelled along the Silk Road, though Xingiang Airlines is probably a new supplier.

We cycled from Kashgar in western China to Gilgit, which is in the heart of the Hunza Valley in Pakistan, which is part of the ancient Silk Road that linked Asia with Europe. For years I had dreamed of cycling along a road filled with caravans going west with porcelain, silk tea, and spices, as wool, gold, ivory and walnuts came from the opposite direction. But I was 500 years too late; the road became redundant when Portuguese seafarer, Vasco da Gama discovered the sea route to Asia round Africa. In the 1960s Pakistan and China built the Karakoram Highway as a gesture of friendship between the two countries, but in many stretches, the road and scenery are desolate.

250 g long grain rice
100g dried apricots
100g raisins
100 g almonds, slivered
2 tbsps peppercorns
salt
yoghurt to taste

Bring a pan of water to the boil. Add a handful of peppercorns and salt to the water. The peppercorns give a spicy edge to what could be a bland dish. Add rice, return to boil, then put the lid on the pan and remove from the heat and leave for 10 minutes; the rice will cook by absorbing the water and removes the risk of the rice catching on the bottom of the pan. Add chopped apricots, raisins, almonds and stir in the yoghurt to coat the grains and serve. Best served as an accompaniment to barbecued meals or grilled vegetables, excellent with lamb kebabs.

Sri Lankan Cashew Nut Curry

This creamy, coconut, protein-packed recipe comes from Browns Beach Hotel, Negombo, in Sri Lanka. I spent a blissful week eating great food and buying gorgeous textiles in this mango-shaped island south of India. In April and May cashews are in season in Sri Lanka so the fresh nuts are soft. If you soak nuts you buy in the supermarket overnight, it should give the nuts a straight-off-the-tree texture. Sri Lanka's beaches are edged with coconut palms and coconut is a favourite ingredient because it tempers the chilli hotness of the curries.

250 g raw cashew nuts soaked in cold water overnight
1-2 tbsps vegetable oil
1 medium onion, chopped
2 garlic cloves, finely grated
2 tsps fresh ginger, finely grated
1 tsp fenugreek seeds
2 tsps ground coriander
1 tsp cumin powder
2 cloves
2 cardamom pods
salt to taste
1 cinnamon stick
600 ml coconut milk

Heat the oil and fry the onions, garlic and ginger until golden. Mix the rest of the ingredients except the coconut milk into the onion mixture and cook for about 10 minutes, stirring continuously to prevent it from sticking. Add coconut milk and bring to a boil, reduce heat and simmer for 5 to 10 minutes. Serve with rice.

Indian Mango Chutney

Chutney is an Indian word derived from the Sanskrit word *chatni,* meaning "for licking." Chutney is basically a spicy side dish that contains fruit or vegetables, vinegar, sugar and spices.

Most local Indian restaurants in India don't serve mango chutney, it is a relish enjoyed in the Indian home, yet no self-respecting poppodam is served without this sweet hot relish outside the subcontinent. There is no reason to resort to the bottled stuff, as it is blissfully easy to make at home, especially with a microwave.

4 roughly chopped fresh mangos
1 1/2 tbsps chopped fresh ginger
2 cloves garlic
1 cinnamon stick
4 whole cloves
1/2 tsp mixed spice powder
60 ml cider vinegar
170 g brown sugar

Chuck mangos into a large microwave-proof bowl with ginger, garlic, cinnamon stick, cloves, mixed spice, cider vinegar and brown sugar. Cover and cook on HIGH for 30 minutes, stir and cook on LOW for 10 minutes until thick and dark brown. If you haven't a microwave: cook for 1 hour in a pan over a low heat. Allow to cool and serve – makes 1 jar.

EAT COOK FEEL GOOD

If the scales veer off too much to the right, if it's 30 degrees centigrade and 90 per cent humidity, these recipes are a welcome relief. Many Asian-inspired salads are very satisfying, as well as being good for you. They draw on interesting spices and herbs, which means there is less of a need for fats and salt for flavour.

Caesar Salad

Caesar Cardini is not a name that trips off the tongue, but his salad definitely does. Cardini was an Italian chef who owned a restaurant in Tijuana, Mexico, and one day in 1924, he threw together this now world-famous, best-dressed collection of leaves – a mix of pungent anchovy mayonnaise, croutons and lettuce.

Conrad International's Italian Nicholini's claims to be the only restaurant in Hong Kong that prepares Caesar salad at your table. I sat back and enjoyed the show; it felt like watching a television cookery programme. The waiter wheeled over the Caesar salad trolley and mixed the salad on the spot in a 1970s-style retro wooden bowl. All the ingredients had been prepared beforehand in little bowls; he cracked a raw egg and blended the egg yolk with mayonnaise, then mashed it with anchovy, salt and pepper. The torn Romaine leaves were tossed with finely grated Parmesan and croutons. Then one dressed leaf was presented on a fork on the plate for sampling – rather like a newly opened bottle of wine.

First make the croutons: Preheat the oven to 180° C. Melt butter with olive oil and halved garlic cloves in a small saucepan; salt and pepper to taste over moderately low heat. Remove the mixture from the heat. Let it stand for 10 minutes, then discard the garlic. In a bowl, toss cubes of Italian or French bread with the butter mixture; spread cubes on a baking sheet and bake in the middle of the oven for 12 to 15 minutes, or until they are golden.

For the dressing: Chop anchovy fillets, and mash with garlic cloves. Then whisk with sherry vinegar, fresh lemon juice, optional raw egg yolk, Worcestershire sauce and dry mustard. Add olive oil in a stream, whisking until the dressing is emulsified.

Remove any brown outer Romaine lettuce leaves. Cut a V into the bottom to take out the root end, which has a bitter taste. Then slice it all the way down into long strips and then go back and cut the strips into squares. Put cut lettuce in the sink with some lukewarm water for about 10 minutes (this expands the cells to make lettuce extra crispy). Shake the water off, and put it in the refrigerator for about a half an hour to an hour to make leaves nice and cold. In a large bowl toss the lettuce leaves with the croutons and the dressing until the salad is combined well and sprinkle the salad with the Parmesan curls.

Croutons:
2 tbsps unsalted butter
2 tbsps olive oil
2 garlic cloves
salt and pepper
750 g of 2 cm cubes of
Italian or French bread

Dressing:
6 flat anchovy fillets, rinsed
and drained
4 garlic cloves
2 tsps sherry vinegar
2 tsps fresh lemon juice
1 raw egg yolk (omit if
serving salad to anyone
elderly or pregnant)
1 tsp Worcestershire sauce
1/2 tsp dry mustard
60 ml olive oil

4 heads of Romaine lettuce
Parmesan curls – buy a big
hunk and curl using a vegetable peeler

Courgette Salad

I had this deceptively easy to
make salad from the antipasti
set lunch buffet at The
Century Hotel's Pepino's New
York/Italian style restaurant.

Ingredients per person:
200 g courgettes
lemon juice to taste
10 g Parmesan cheese
2 tbsps olive oil
salt and pepper

Wash the courgettes, there is
no need to peel them; finely
grate. Put in a salad bowl; add
lemon juice, olive oil, salt and
pepper. Finally, pare thin
slices of cheese using a vegetable
peeler; sprinkle on top and
serve.

73

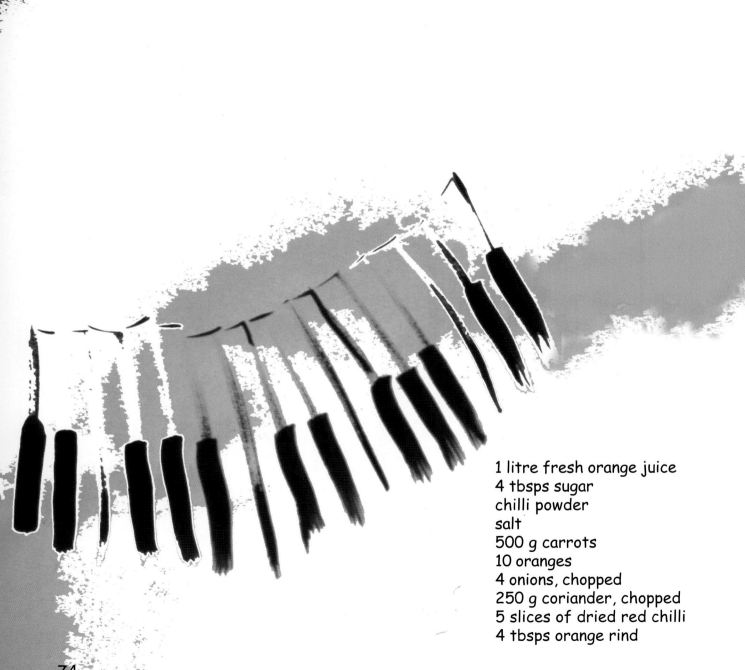

1 litre fresh orange juice
4 tbsps sugar
chilli powder
salt
500 g carrots
10 oranges
4 onions, chopped
250 g coriander, chopped
5 slices of dried red chilli
4 tbsps orange rind

Orange & Carrot Salad

Chef Roberto Treves and Chef Sergio Snyder of "Magallanica" restaurant in Mexico City have appointed themselves ambassadors of Mexican cooking and they rove round the world creating Mexican dishes and music. Chef Sergio owns a banquet catering service and is a cooking teacher as well as a restaurant consultant. He studied architecture and graduated from the Juilliard School of Music, then proceeded to become a concert-pianist in New York. He learnt to cook from his grandmother who taught him old Mexican recipes.

The Mexican chefs were 'playing' Café Vienna in the Holiday Inn Golden Mile. Roving in between the experienced buffet loaders and tourists, the pair stood out as two flamboyant figures clad in bright ponchos, sombreros and black trousers adorned with silver ornaments. They alternated between enthusiastic piano playing, maraca shaking and dispensing advice on Mexican dishes. I loved this incredibly refreshing orange and carrot salad.

Peel the carrots and cut into long rods, as if making carrot sticks for a dip. Bring the fresh orange juice with sugar to a boil; add chilli powder and salt to taste. Boil for 3 minutes, then add half the carrot sticks. Cook for another 3 minutes, then drain the carrots. Mix the cooked carrot strips with the other half of the raw, chunky carrot sticks. Peel the oranges and cut them into cubes, discarding any pith. Add the oranges, onions, coriander, red chilli and orange rind.

Pomelo Salad

I first had this salad at the Oriental Bangkok. The pomelo is a great new fruit discovery for me, as it has the sweet juiciness of an orange and the citrus kick of a grapefruit, but without the bitterness. The pomelo is a native of Thailand and Malaysia. A good pomelo has a smooth yellow-green skin and is firm but not hard. To attack it – cut off the thick, quilted skin, pull apart the segments and gently remove the outer covering. The pulpy segments will stay fresh for up to 3 days if kept in the refrigerator. In Chinese the word for pomelo sounds like "blessing," and the fruit is considered auspicious – especially at Chinese New Year. Pomelos are usually sold in the shops and markets all the year round. The pink ones tend to have more juice and are more expensive, but watch out for large light ones as the flesh tends to be dry. Despite being such a large fruit, the size is deceptive in terms of yield, so don't stint on lugging back more pomelos than you think to make this salad.

1 tin of coconut milk
100 g minced pork
2 tbsps chilli jam
(Naam Prig Paa)
100 g minced prawns
1 tbsp palm sugar
2 tbsps fish sauce
2 tbsps lime juice
flesh from 3 to 4 pomelos
100 g good quality
frozen cooked prawns (with
tails still on)
meat from one young,
fresh coconut
shredded chillies to decorate

Don't shake the can of coconut milk –
pour off the thick milk and leave the
watery liquid in the can. Heat the
thick milk with the minced pork. Add
the chilli jam (available from Thai
groceries in Wanchai or a Chinese
version of soy chilli jam from
Wellcome), minced prawns, palm
sugar, fish sauce and lime juice. Cook
for 5 minutes. Leave to cool. Add the
flesh from the pomelo, the defrosted
prawns and the coconut meat. Save a
few prawns and some coconut for
decoration. Scatter a few chillies on
top and serve in a halved pomelo.

Papaya Body Rub

While staying at the Oriental, I took the hotel boat over to the Hotel Spa for a herbal Thai treatment. I felt as a food person I should try one of the Thai food-related treatments: the papaya body polish. Papaya has an enzyme called papain that breaks down fibres and is used as a meat tenderiser; I was quite intrigued to see the results (two thirds of papaya usage in the USA is as a meat tenderiser and it is also used as a beer stabilising agent). My whole body was smeared with warm, liquefied papaya, then wrapped in a plastic sheet and towels. I was left to 'tenderise' for half an hour while my head was gently massaged. Then I was unmummified and quite relieved that my skin did not fall off my bones. In terms of texture, my skin did seem a bit smoother, though my white t-shirt took on an orange hue. If you ever have a glut of papayas, it's worth trying this body wrap at home.

Liquidise papaya and warm gently in a pan; make sure it's not too hot. Apply liberally.

Cajun Pumpkin & Sweet Potato Salad

This salad is a long-standing favourite at the Continental restaurant in Quarry Bay. It is not labour intensive to make, but does require time to bake the vegetables in the oven.

700 g pumpkin
500 g sweet potato
4 pieces spring onion
350 g corn kernels, frozen
or canned
1 red pepper
1 red dried chilli

Dressing (adjust quantities to taste)
4 tbsps olive oil
1 tsp Dijon mustard
1 tsp mustard seed, fried
1 tbsp red wine vinegar
salt and pepper
1 tsp brown sugar

Peel and cut pumpkin into chunks, bake pieces in a medium oven until still firm. While the oven is on, bake whole dried chilli, then scrape out seeds. Peel potato and cut into chunky slices; char-grill till marked with black criss-crosses, then bake in oven for 30 minutes. Chop spring onion, red pepper and chilli; mix all ingredients together. Make dressing and toss all together.

Ronda's Fabulous Flapjacks
(wheat/dairy allergy-free)

Whenever I went round to a friend's house she always had the most delicious flapjacks on offer. Then she discovered her flapjack-loving daughter Cordelia was allergic to wheat and dairy products, so her helper Ronda adapted the recipe and now they taste even better. If wheat is not a problem in your life, then substitute both the soya and rice flours for 300 g of self-raising flour, omit the baking soda and use butter if you love dairy.

300 g polysaturated margarine
300 g rolled oats
250 g raisins
200 g chopped apricots
110 g castor sugar
150 g soya flour
150 g rice flour
3 level tsps baking soda
3 tbsps honey
3 tbsps golden syrup

Grease 30 cm x 20 cm cake tin and line with greaseproof paper. Mix all ingredients together and press into tin. Bake for 20 minutes in a medium hot oven (about 180° C) until lightly golden.

Strawberries in Red Wine

Forget the traditional marriage of strawberries and cream. The red wine or vinegar actually enhances the strawberry flavour rather that beat it into a cholesterol and sugar submission.

Ingredients:
fresh, hulled strawberries
red wine or balsamic vinegar
castor sugar
mint leaves

Marinate the strawberries to taste in either the red wine or the balsamic vinegar and sugar for several hours in the fridge, serve chilled, garnished with mint leaves.

EAT COOK DRINK

Break the ice in more ways than one - from high-class cocktails to refreshing lassis and spicy tea.

Crème de Cassis Cocktail

Crème de cassis is a thick blackcurrant alcoholic spirit made by soaking blackcurrants in alcohol, which is then sweetened with sugar. Don't underestimate its alcoholic qualities – 20 per cent volume. Hong Kong wine shops sell crème de cassis for about $150 per bottle. The most popular way of drinking this liqueur is in a Kir cocktail (1 part crème de cassis to 4 parts dry wine or if it's sparkling wine it's a Kir Royale). The cocktail gets its name from a crème de cassis-loving priest called Felix Kir. As a reward for his work as a resistance fighter in the Second World War, Kir was made mayor of Dijon. Kir was known for only serving crème de cassis and wine at all the official receptions in Dijon.

Not that I am advocating creating drinks on the cheap, but if you have a spare bottle of vodka, you could try making your own cassis: cook 370 g blackcurrants in 750 ml boiling water for about 5 minutes; allow to cool and discard the water. Put the currants in a bottle of vodka and steep for 1 to 2 weeks, while occasionally shaking the jar vigorously. Strain and filter through a fine cloth. Add 125 ml sugar syrup, stir and taste.

This crème de cassis cocktail is surprisingly refreshing; the freshly squeezed lemon juice is the perfect foil to the rich blackcurrant syrup. If you mix it with soda water, it's a drink that's rather too easy to drink. It is also a nice cocktail to adapt for teetotallers as you can substitute blackcurrant cordial so they do not look like obvious abstainers.

On no account use bought squeezed lemon juice. Mix with soda water and add crème de cassis to taste - it produces a gorgeous crimson swirl. Add ice cubes and top with mint leaves.

1 part crème de cassis
3 parts soda water
1 part fresh lemon juice
fresh mint

Platinum Journey Cocktail

The Platinum Journey cocktail – a heady concoction of vodka, cointreau and sherry and lime juice – is a Peninsula Hotel favourite. After some very enjoyable experimenting at home, I found it tastes even better if you use freshly squeezed lime juice rather than the bought stuff. If it is too sour, just add some more sherry or make a syrup by dissolving 2 tbsps of sugar in 6 tbsps of water. For a more immediate trial, the Platinum Journey is available at all Peninsula outlets.

1 1/2 part Absolut Citron vodka
1/2 part Tio Pepe sherry
1/2 part cointreau
1/2 part Roses lime juice
3 parts Bitter Lemon
lime slices

Shake top 4 ingredients well with ice cubes and pour into a glass. Top off with Bitter Lemon and garnish with freshly cut lime slices.

The Perfect Martini

Tango Martini is located on the third floor of an office building in Wan Chai, and is not the most obvious place to find a Martini bar. This former Rugby Union Club is fitted out with huge fake-fur tiger and zebra sofas and armchairs so you are practically horizontal before you even have a drink. Big candles flicker round the lounge, dining area (there is a simple Mediterranean menu and the most gorgeous artery-clogging, stomach-lining French cheese plate) and cigar lounge.

There are several stories about the origins of the Martini. Citizens of Martinez, California, claimed that around 1870 a bar on Ferry Street in Martinez was serving up a whisky-based cocktail with an olive. An Italian immigrant bartender called Martini de Teggia in New York in the 1900's claimed that he made a drink that included dry gin, dry vermouth and orange bitters. According to British cocktail lore, the drink's name derived from the Martini & Henry rifle used by the British army between 1871 and 1891. It's not clear whether they were stirring the drink with the rifle, or shaking for fear of it. The first mention of the word Martini (made with sweet gin) was in the *New and Improved Illustrated Bartender's Manual* on *How to Mix Drinks of the Present Style* published by Harry Johnson in 1888. By the turn of the century, a flurry of American bar manuals contained a recipe for the Martini that had been simplified to just sweet vermouth and gin in equal parts with an optional dash of orange bitters. The word Martini was by now in common usage among bartenders on both sides of the Atlantic.

To make the ultimate Martini, keep your glasses and even your shaker in the freezer until you are ready to begin. Only use glass and stainless steel shakers for mixing and drinking. Be careful when shaking – over shake and you will just end up diluting your drink. If you are using olives as garnish, rinse them under water just before you put them into the Martini so the olive juice doesn't leave an oil slick on your drink. Stirring with ice leaves the drink absolutely clear, but Bond apparently preferred the misty effect and extra chill obtained by shaking.

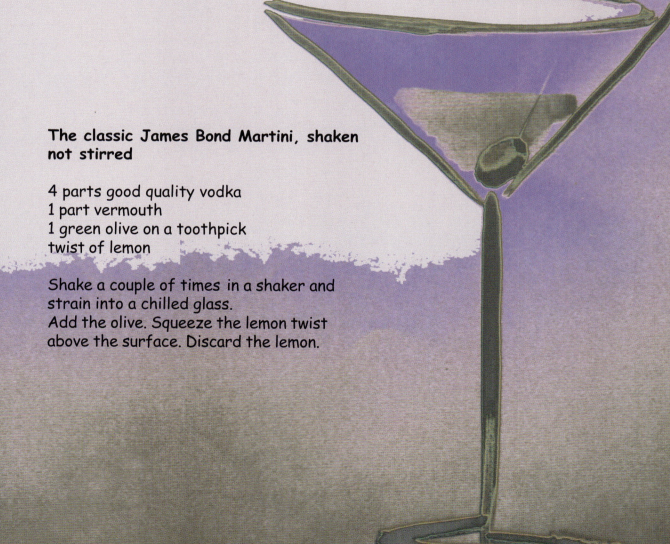

The classic James Bond Martini, shaken not stirred

4 parts good quality vodka
1 part vermouth
1 green olive on a toothpick
twist of lemon

Shake a couple of times in a shaker and strain into a chilled glass.
Add the olive. Squeeze the lemon twist above the surface. Discard the lemon.

Rugby Sevens Cocktail Jellies

For pre-, post- and during Rugby Sevens gatherings, here are some interesting and novel ways to increase your alcohol consumption. Based on the vodka jelly shot – well known at Al's Diner, Lan Kwai Fong – jelly shots can be easily made at home. They're easy to transport once they're set; a great way to have a user-friendly, quick burst of alcohol whenever your energy is flagging or sobriety is threatening. Robertsons' an SAR-based company make 13 different flavours of jelly powder, sold in most main supermarkets. The creative challenge is to mix and match the jelly powders and alcohol to make cocktail jellies. Experiment with flavours such as cola, piña colada, lime, passionfruit, lychee, orange, banana, mango, pineapple and strawberry. A few obvious ones are cola jelly and Jack Daniels' piña colada jelly and light rum. Some interesting variations I have discovered are:

Strawberry daiquiri: strawberry jelly, light rum and raspberry liqueur
Screwdriver: orange jelly and vodka
Sex on the beach: pineapple jelly, crème de cassis and Midori melon liqueur
Margarita: lemon jelly, fresh lime juice (to taste), tequila and Triple Sec or other orange liqueur.

Makes 10 half egg-shaped jellies

90 g packet Robertsons' jelly flavoured powder
100 ml spirits
100 ml boiling water
100 ml cold water
2 plastic egg boxes
cocktail sticks

Empty the jelly powder into a bowl, add boiling water to the powder and stir vigorously until the liquid is clear, then add alcohol. To speed up setting, add 5 ice cubes instead of cold water. For stiffer jelly use less water. Pour liquid into the egg cartons. You can use any small container, but egg cartons are easy to transport. Put in fridge, not the freezer as freezing breaks down the water molecules and the jelly becomes cloudy. Allow about 1 hour to set and serve with cocktails sticks.

Traditional Indian Tea

You are never far from a cup of hot, spicy, sweet milky chai in India and Pakistan. Within a 5-minute radius or even closer there is guaranteed to be a big pot boiling with tea leaves, milk and spices. The most incredible tea experience I had was in Gilgit, Pakistan; there was a tiny shop in an alley and an old man sitting cross legged beside a huge pot boiling with fresh black tea leaves, milk, sugar, cardamom, fresh ginger and desiccated coconut, which gave a natural sweetness to the spicy brew. Chai is now being marketed as aggressively as coffee and you can buy cold or hot chai blends in many coffee shops. But it is worth knowing how to make your own. The best place to buy your spices is the ground floor of Chung King Mansions and also on the ground floor the Taj Mahal Club Mess, which sells delicately scented cardamom and ginger tea in a Styrofoam cup for less than $5.

200 ml water
1 cardamom pod
fresh ginger
1-2 big size whole black peppercorns
4 cloves
zest from 1 orange
1 cinnamon stick
2 tsps desiccated coconut
125 ml semi-skimmed milk
1 full tsp black tea
sugar to taste

Heat water with cardamom, fresh ginger, black peppercorns, cloves, orange zest, cinnamon stick and desiccated coconut in a pan. Cook for about 15 minutes, stirring continuously. Add the milk and simmer again. Throw in the tea leaves, cover the pan and turn off the heat. After 2 minutes, strain the tea into cups and serve immediately. The coconut adds a sweetness of its own and means less sugar is needed, if at all.

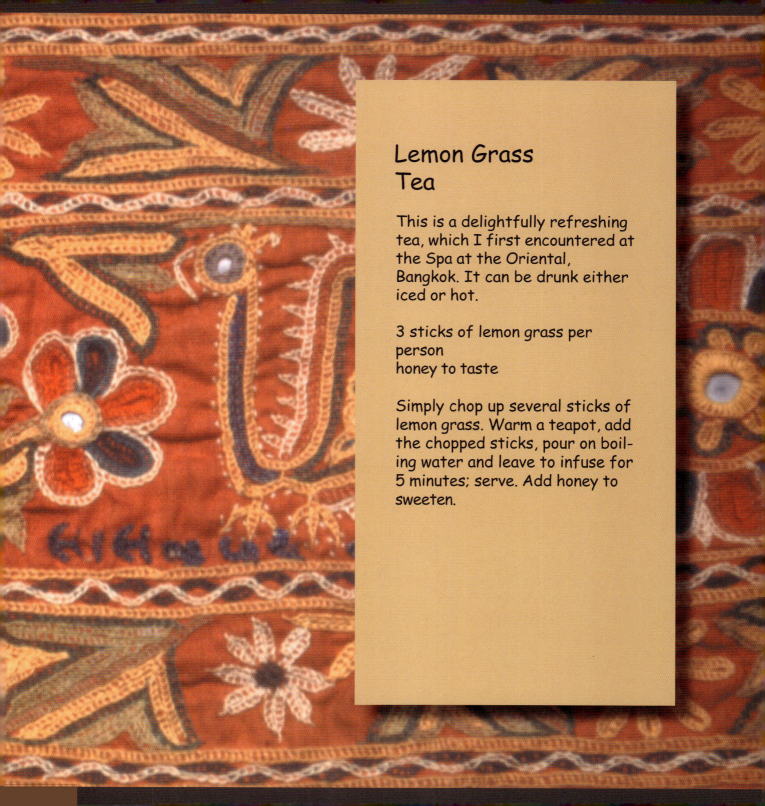

Lemon Grass Tea

This is a delightfully refreshing tea, which I first encountered at the Spa at the Oriental, Bangkok. It can be drunk either iced or hot.

3 sticks of lemon grass per person
honey to taste

Simply chop up several sticks of lemon grass. Warm a teapot, add the chopped sticks, pour on boiling water and leave to infuse for 5 minutes; serve. Add honey to sweeten.

Lassis

Lassis are yoghurt drinks which can be drunk either plain, salted or with fresh fruit. They are a natural thirst quencher in hot countries and the only way of 'putting out the fire' after eating a chilli hot curry. Yoghurt should be 'live,' which means it still contains the bacteria lactobacillus acidophilus that helps to maintain a healthy intestinal tract essential for digestion and good health. Yoghurt can be made from any milk – sheep, cow, goat and even soy. To save calories, it also works with skimmed milk.

1 litre of milk
4 tsps live bought yoghurt

Heat milk to blood temperature; your finger should be able to withstand the heat. Whisk in the bought yoghurt culture and leave for 12 hours in a warm place – an oven with just the electric light turned on will provide sufficient heat or even a sunny window ledge. Take care it sets, but does not separate. When it is set, store in the fridge. It will be runnier than the usual bought stuff. For thicker yoghurt you can add 1 tsp of milk powder with the culture. To make your fruit lassi, blend yoghurt with a little syrup, ice and fruit of your choice; banana is a good option as is mango. Lemon juice is also a refreshing blend.

Hong Kong Restaurant Guide

Thank you to the restaurants that very kindly allowed me to print their recipes in *Eat Cook Hong Kong*. Here is where to find them. I have also included restaurants and bars I think are interesting and offer a unique Hong Kong dining/drinking experience.

A

Al's Diner, 27-39 D'Aguilar Street, Central
Telephone: 2869 1869
Great for late night jello shots – or make your own. See vodka jellies recipe page 90.

American Peking, 20 Lockhart Road, Wan Chai
Telephone: 2527 1000
American Peking serves authentic Peking food, which is a rich, slightly spicy, oily, noodle/bread-based cuisine. Peking duck recipe page 12.

Aqua, 49 Hollywood Road, Central
Telephone 2545 9889
They have a modern Australian menu with Asian twists

B

The Bayou, 4-13 Shelley Street, Mid-Levels
Telephone: 2574 5046
Friendly Cajun restaurant which looks on to the escalator. Serves up portions big enough to give you the energy to pick a whole field of cotton. Sweet potato pie recipe page 28.

C

Café des Artistes, 30-32 D'Aguilar Street, Central
Telephone: 2526 3880
Super enthusiastic French/Italian Chef Bagnato dishes up French classics with a twist.

Caramba, 26-30 Elgin Street, SoHo
Telephone: 2530 9963
Jolly, good value TexMex food; great Margaritas made with fresh lime juice.

The Century Hotel's Pepino's Cucina Italiana, 1/F, 238 Jaffe Road, Wan Chai
Telephone: 2598 8888
Good value Italian food. Courgette salad recipe page 73.

China Tee Club, 101 Pedder Building, 12 Pedder Street, Central
Telephone: 2521 0233
Whirring ceiling fans, lush palm trees, big windows with shutters, delicate marble tables – all in the heart of Central. Great place to go for scones, cakes and dim sum savouries, and also for buckets of Chinese/English tea and non-stop gossip.

Cococabana, House 7 Mo Tat Wan, Lamma
Telephone: 2328 2138
Escape to the Med at this restaurant by the beach. They have good, well-cooked dishes; the fish soup alone is worth the boat ride from Aberdeen.

The Continental, 2 Hoi Wan Street, Quarry Bay
Telephone: 2563 2209
Good salads and great cakes. Chocolate marble cheesecake recipe page 31; Cajun pumpkin and sweet potato salad recipe page 78.

E

Elgin Tastes, 38 Elgin Street, SoHo
Telephone: 2810 5183
Goldfish bowl dining experience – big plate-glass windows and white interiors. Modern Australian food. Orange and almond cake with orange and cardamom ice cream recipe page 52 .

F

Feather Boa, 38 Staunton Street, SoHo
Telephone: 2857 2586
An antique shop turned bar. Sink into a deep, embroidered sofa and a generous gin and tonic.

G

Grand Hyatt Hotel, 1 Harbour Road, Wan Chai
Telephone: 2861 1234
The ground floor Coffee Shop offers interesting food throughout the day. The excellent Italian restaurant Grissini on the second floor welcomes you with a Grissini machine discharging hot bread sticks from the oven at the entrance. Tuna salad recipe page 47; Brie and walnut pancakes recipe page 25.

H

Han Lok Yuen Pigeon, 16-17 Hung Shing Yea, Lamma
> Telephone: 2982 0680
> This charming, red-walled, indoor and outdoor restaurant is perched on a hill overlooking Power Station beach. Minced quail recipe page 19.

Holiday Inn, Café Vienna,
> Golden Mile's 50 Nathan Road, Tsim Sha Tsui
> Telephone: 2315 1118
> From this all-rounder Café: Mexican orange and carrot salad recipe page 74. The Avenue, which is the Holiday Inn's signature restaurant, dishes up some stylish dishes.

I

Indochine 1929, 2/F, California Tower,
> 30-32 D'Aguilar Street, Central
> Telephone: 2869 7399
> Old-style lamps, palm trees, ceiling fans and cane furniture take you back to 1920's Vietnam. Fresh spring rolls and Hanoi fish are recommended. Finish off with coffee in a Vietnamese filter served with condensed milk.

K

La Kasbah, Basement 17, Hollywood Road, Central
> Telephone: 2525 9493
> It's North African with carpets, dark red walls, candles, couscous, preserved lemons and mint tea.

L

Lucy's Restaurant, G/F, 64 Stanley Main Street, Stanley
> Telephone: 2813 9055
> Intimate ground-floor restaurant with inspiring international menu. Peppercorn meringue recipe page 51.

M

M at the Fringe, 2 Lower Albert Road, Central
> Telephone: 2877 4000
> Great individual décor and food to match: slow cooked lamb, suckling pig and Pavlova – always a worthwhile stimulating experience.

Mak's Noodle, 77 Wellington Street, Central
> Telephone: 2854 3810
> Fast, flavour-packed won tons served in a peppery broth.

Mandarin Oriental Hotel, 5 Connaught Road, Central
> Telephone: 2522 0111
> The first floor Chinnery Bar has great warming pies and casseroles and a good selection of malt whiskys, Vong is a top-floor harbour-view restaurant with exotic French and Thai combinations. Warm chocolate pudding is a must, as is the refreshing ginger and lemon grass soda. Rich chocolate brownies are available at most outlets and in the Mandarin Cakeshop. Brownie recipe page 32.

Martino Coffee Shop, 66 Paterson Street, Causeway Bay
> At the Victoria Harbour end of Paterson Street look for the giant coffee pot billowing out steam above the entrance. Martino has the atmosphere of an international, seedy coffee den in some Eastern European capital with creamy, smoked walls; dark wood and orange swivel chairs like waltzer chairs. There is a wide selection of freshly brewed coffees, but the highlight for me is the alcoholic coffees. Cointreau Coffee is prepared at your table. The Cointreau is heated in a spoon with a strip of orange peel, then set alight to make a blue flame. The flaming liquid is added to the freshly percolated coffee, then fresh cream is spooned on top. Refills are half price; you could easily stay there all night, at least until midnight when the giant coffee pot outside steams its last puff.

Milano, 2/F, Sun Hung Kai Centre, 30 Harbour Road, Wan Chai
> Telephone: 2598 1222
> This is an Italian restaurant with harbour views. Cappuccino crème brulée recipe page 50.

Ming Kee restaurant, Po Toi Island
> Telephone: 2849 7038
> Al fresco seafood dining and excellent deep-fried squid. Deep-fried squid recipe page 18.

Moon Garden, 5 Hoi Ping Road, Causeway Bay
> Telephone: 2882 6878
> Gorgeous, old-style Chinese tea house with a selection of over 70 teas. Blissfully easy to spend a couple of hours drinking endless bowls of tea and playing Chinese checkers.

N

Nicholini's Conrad International, 8/F, Pacific Place
Telephone: 2521 3838
Very smart Italian restaurant with Italian chef and many imported Italian ingredients. Caesar salad is made at the table. Caesar salad recipe page 72.

P

Panevino, 11 Mosque Junction, Mid-Levels
Telephone: 2521 7366
This is an intimate Italian restaurant with great bread and pasta.

The Peak Café, 121 Peak Road, The Peak
Telephone: 2849 7868
This was originally a workshop for engineers working on the Peak Tram, which opened in 1888. This lovely, old building has indoor and outdoor restaurants; in the winter there are braziers to keep warm and in the summer there is always a gentle breeze in the lush garden. Live jazz is played in the garden on certain nights.

Petrus, 56/F, Shangri-La Hotel, Supreme Court Road, Admiralty
Telephone: 2820 8590
Tiptop French cuisine at equally high prices in an opulent setting with opulent food. I love the guinea fowl pie with cep mushrooms and chestnuts served with a black truffle sauce. A cheese buyer for some of the top Paris restaurants selects the cheese so there is a range of very unusual as well as familiar French cheeses. The 5 or 6 course set menu is a good value way to enjoy Petrus.

The Peninsula Hotel, Salisbury Road, Kowloon
Telephone: 2315 3171
Great Lobby for eating scones and jam and for an Asian twist on Afternoon Tea. The first floor Chinese 1930s-style restaurant Spring Moon has a wide range of Chinese teas and afternoon snacks. Sushi recipe page 56; Platinum Cocktail recipe page 88.

Pitta Place, Shop 75, Chungking Mansion6, 36-44 Nathan Road, Kowloon
Telephone: 2369 3288
Marinated lamb or chicken freshly cut off the rotating spit is stuffed into a pitta pocket with a garlicky lemon sauce. The original owner Tunisian Rafet Azaiez fell in love with a Hong Kong music teacher while travelling in Europe. They settled here and he opened up this tiny shop. Though they've sold the Pitta Place, it is still as popular.

La Placita, 13/F, Food Forum, Times Square, Causeway Bay
Telephone: 2506 3308
This TexMex restaurant with good margaritas is handy to the Times Square cinemas. The Mexican staff at the Consulate say they buy their tortillas here, which are handmade.

Post 97, 9-11 Lan Kwai Fong, Central
Telephone: 2186 1816
When you can't decide what to eat and where to eat, Post 97 always has something to suit your mood from eggs benedict to nachos to fat chips.

R

The Regent Hotel, 18 Salisbury Road, Kowloon
Telephone: 2721 1211
Yu Seafood restaurant has good seafood choices, a great setting and a giant fish tank entrance. Tomato and gin mousse recipe page 41 from the European restaurant Plume, also in the Regent Hotel.

Le Rendezvous, G/F, 5 Staunton Street, SoHo
Telephone: 2905 1808
They serve freshly made Breton-style crepes in a very intimate atmosphere.

Revolving 66, 62/F, Hopewell Centre, 183 Queen's Road East, Wan Chai
Telephone: 2862 6166
It's enough to make your head spin; have a cocktail at the revolving bar and in 66 minutes, you'll see a complete revolution of Hong Kong.

S

Staunton's Wine Bar and Café, 10-12 Staunton Street, Central
Telephone: 2973 6611
This location is great for people watching. Get a table by the street or escalator and order a tall, hot latte or a good, thin crust pizza. They have a wide range of wines available by the glass.

T

Taj Mahal Club Mess, Chungking Mansions,
36-44 Nathan Road, Kowloon
Telephone: 2722 5454
This is just one of the many adequate Indian restaurants in the Mansions. They sell delicately scented cardamom and ginger tea in a Styrofoam cup for less than $5 from the ground-floor restaurant.

Tango Martini, 3/F, Empire Land Commercial Centre,
81-85 Lockhart Road, Wan Chai
Telephone: 2528 0855
They have fabulous martinis served up in a fake-fur setting. Martini recipe page 88.

Thai Basil Bar Café, Shop 005, LG Pacific Place,
88 Queensway
Telephone: 2537 4682
This restaurant located in the basement is a sleek, modern Thai restaurant with stunning presentation and interesting combinations of flavours and textures. Coconut prawns with ginger lime drizzle recipe page 42; Sticky banana pudding recipe page 35.

Tott's Asian Grill & Bar, 34/F, The Excelsior,
281 Gloucester Road, Causeway Bay
Telephone: 2837 6786
The harbour is at your fork with great views and interesting food from the open kitchen. Artichoke Parma ham rolls recipe page 40.

Tung's Kitchen, 32-34 Lock Road, Tsim Sha Tsui
Telephone: 2191 9928
This busy restaurant serves up Chiu Chow food – sea moss, rose buds and oyster congee.

U

Uncle Willie's Deli, 36 Wyndham Street, Central
Telephone: 2522 7524
Salads, smoothies and fantastic cakes – Chocolate Cloud Cake is a solid, dense chocolate cake topped with cream that is worth getting fat for. You'll have to buy it at the Deli because they refuse to give away the recipe. You can also buy the cakes, quiches and breads from the Staunton Street Patisserie. Broccoli frittata recipe page 26.

W

Wing Xai Yuen Szechuan Noodle Shop,
Diamond Hill MTR, exit C2
A telephone number is difficult to locate, but finding this place will be well worth your time. In Diamond Hill there is a 50-year-old squatter village of ramshackle corrugated iron huts that will soon be flattened for redevelopment. Within this labyrinth of old iron is a number of restaurants, presumably started by the immigrants who first settled here. One of the most famous is the Wing Xai Yuen Szechuan Noodle Shop. Cross the flyover and weave your way past drying clothes and medicinal herbs. Ignore any restaurants that are not packed until you get to the bottom of the lane; Wing Xai has red, iron gates that are open. Walk past the tiny dim sum baskets full of steamed dishes and squeeze into a narrow booth or opt for a bigger, round table. The walls are decorated with Chinese writing and red, paper lanterns. Most people are slurping noodles, which swim in a sea of rich vermilion red, spicy peanut broth. Three of us divided a large bowl; the best bit is at the bottom when you hit the sludgy peanut. You can also enjoy a few Szechuan favourites: four season beans; spicy, long green beans; great chunks of eggplant in a rich tomato spicy sauce; bamboo shoots and steamed chicken with garlic. Dishes have enough edge to them without bringing tears to the eye. There is a shortened menu in English.

Z

Zahra, 409A Jaffe Road, Wan Chai
Telephone: 2838 4597
This tiny Middle Eastern restaurant consistently serves up stunning, fresh tasting herb- and spice-laden dishes. A mezze plate is a good introduction to Zahra's menu.

Cooking Classes

Taking a cooking class is a fun way to increase your cooking confidence and to learn new techniques. Some courses just offer demonstrations with a chance to taste at the end - while others involve rolling up the sleeves and getting flour under your fingernails.

In Hong Kong:

Chopsticks Cooking Centre
8 Soares Avenue, Kowloon
Telephone: 2336 8433
They offer Chinese and international cooking lessons with demonstration and practical lessons. The focus is on Chinese dishes; deep-fried bean curd fingers, carrot carving, shrimp dumplings and won ton soup.

The Home Management Centre
10/F, Electric Centre, 28 Garden Road, North Point
Telephone: 2510 2828
The Centre offers Chinese home-cooking courses throughout the year. The 6-class course includes dishes such as chicken with walnuts, egg fu-yung, spring rolls and minced meat with broccoli. There are also Thai and French cooking classes available.

The Island School Evening Institute
20 Borrett Road, Mid-Levels
Telephone: 2526 5884
The Institute runs demonstration international cooking classes in the evenings; classes run from autumn to spring.

Town Gas Cooking Centre
Leighton Centre, Causeway Bay
Telephone: 2576 1535
The Centre has a wide range of practical and demonstration international cooking lessons. Dishes cooked by participants can be eaten there or taken home.

The YWCA
1 MacDonnell Road, Mid-Levels
Telephone: 2522 4291
The YWCA runs short courses in Western and Asian dishes. Such is the craving for noodle know-how; Oodles of Noodles usually has a waiting list. Classes run from autumn to spring.

Many of the hotels such as The Mandarin, The Ritz-Carlton and The Peninsula run cooking classes from time to time; it's worth asking your favourite hotel restaurant if there are cooking classes in the offing. The Regent will run specially-tailored cooking classes for small groups where you can request for a specific dish to be taught, then eaten for lunch later.

Further afield:

Thailand:

If you can't stand the heat on the Thai beach get into the kitchen: cookery programs are becoming very popular in Thailand.

The Thai Cooking School
The Oriental Hotel, 48 Oriental Avenue, Bangkok 10500
Telephone: (662) 236 0400
This popular programme, which is open to hotel guests and visitors, has been going for more than 15 years. The school is in a delight-ful old building on the opposite bank to the hotel and is reached by the Oriental's complimentary barge. The comprehensive cooking programme consists of 4 mornings of demonstration lessons followed by lunch. The 4-day course covers the main aspects of Thai cuisine. For example, if it's Monday it's snacks and salads, Tuesday is soups and desserts, Wednesday is curries and Thursday is steams, stir-fry and grill dishes.

The Boathouse
2/2 Moo 2, Patak Road, Kata Beach, Phuket
Telephone: (66 76) 330015-17
They offer informal Thai cooking classes every weekend plus a visit to the local market.

The Thai House
32/4 Moo 8 Tambal, Bangmaung, Ampur, Bangyai, Nontaburi
Telephone: (662) 280 0740
A traditional teak guesthouse on a canal, where guests can pick their own Thai herbs in the garden and learn to cook in the outside kitchen.

Bali:

In Bali more hotels and restau-rants are offering not just cooking demonstrations but programmes that incorporate market trips, cooking classes, lunch and dinner, traditional massages and dancing displays.

Ritz-Carlton
Jimbaran, Bali
Telephone: (62) 361 702 222
They offer a two-day cultural programme called *Rasa Bumbu* (*rasa* means spice and *bumbu* means taste in Indonesian). See page 60 for steamed fish baked in a banana leaf as taught at the cooking school.

Janet de Neefe at The Casa Luna Restaurant, Jin, Raya, in Ubud, also offers a three-day cooking class that incorporates classes with trips to the local market.
Telephone: (62) 361 973 283

Shops & Services

Supermarkets:
Most supermarkets are open from 8 am to 10 pm. Some are 24 hour. Depending on where you live and lift-permitting, most supermarkets will deliver. They also have Web sites to make shopping even easier.

city'super
Times Square, Basement One, Causeway Bay
Customer Service Hotline Telephone: 2506-2888
 Harbour City, Level Three, Tsim Sha Tsui
Customer Service Hotline Telephone: 2375-8222
Web site: www.citysuper.com.hk
This is a high-quality, gourmet-oriented supermarket covering a full spectrum of food products imported from all over the world. Products include delicatessen, cheese, confectionery, coffee, tea, grocery, dairy and frozen products, Japanese food and sake, fish, meat, poultry, fruits, vegetables, wine and spirits.

Oliver's Delicatessen
Shop 233, 2/F, Prince's Building, Central
Telephone: 2810 7710
Web site: oliversdeli@dairyfarm.com.hk
Oliver's has wide aisles and well-stocked shelves (i.e. stock on shelves as opposed to blocking the aisles). It is a pleasure to shop in with speciality, up-market produce; fresh bread and roasted chickens from the deli counter. They have 2 other branches.

Park'N Shop
Telephone: 2606 8833 (general office)
This is a supermarket chain widely dispersed through-out Hong Kong that sells international wines and foods; the location of the Park'N Shop will determine the diversity of the produce.

Wellcome
Telephone: 2489 5888 for nearest outlet
There are Wellcome supermarkets all over Hong Kong selling similar produce to Park'N Shop.

Wine:
Supermarkets get big discounts on wine, so they have a wide range of reasonably priced wines. For something less mainstream look for the smaller wine merchants.

Berry Brothers and Rudd
Telephone: 2110 1680
A British-based company selling fine wines in Hong Kong.

Castello del Vino
G/F, 12 Anton Street, Wanchai
Telephone: 2866 0587
Italian deli that sells pastas and fine wines, and also useful things like new rubber rings for espresso machines.

Megareve
Unit 1015 Hing Wan Centre,
7 Tin Wan Praya Road, Aberdeen
Telephone: 2555 1284
This is a French wine wholesale megastore.

Remy Fine Wines
Telephone: 2523 5904 for nearest outlet
There are several branches of this up-market range of wine shops in Hong Kong.

Watson's Wine Cellar
36 Queen's Road Central
Telephone: 2146 3640 (There are other branches.)
Web site: www.watsonwine.com
This location has more than 1,000 wines, beers and spirits from around the world.

Speciality Food Shopping:

Filipino:
On the first floor of Worldwide House, Central, there are tiny shops filled with Filipino groceries and also take-away food such as Adobo – a blood-enriched pork stew –and sticky coconut rice sweets.

Indian:
Indian Provisions Store G/F, 65 -66 Chung King Mansions
With such a dense concentration of Indian restaurants, the turnover is likely to be high; this store is a good source of fresh Indian spices and vegetables.

Indonesian:
In the streets around the Indonesian Consulate on Leighton Road, Causeway Bay, are numerous small shops selling prawn crackers, Redang spice mixes and chicken and rice wrapped in banana leaves to take away.

Spanish:
Fiesta Ltd. 1/F, 13 Li Yuen Street East
Telephone: 2534 6807
You can find Spanish olive oils, cheeses, hams, wines and tinned produce, as well as Spanish pottery and paella pans here.

Thai:
The Thai Classic Thai Food and Grocery Shop
36 Cross Street
Telephone: 2591 5237
This shop is just one of many. Look for the Thai squiggly writing and follow your nose. The essential flavourings in Thai cooking are kaffir lime leaves, which are green glossy leaves shaped like the number eight; zest from the kaffir lime, which has a very distinctive nobbly texture (the juice is too sour and is used as a hair rinse in Thailand); lemon grass; galangal (similar to ginger); green and red chillies; coconut milk; banana leaves and fish sauce. You can usually buy most of these ingredients at the big name supermarkets, but you are better off going for a fresh, very much cheaper option at the Thai supermarkets, which also double as impromptu restaurants.

Organic:

Green Cottage Shop and Co-op
15 A Main St, Yung Shue Wan, Lamma
Telephone: 2982 6934
Fresh breads, juices and organic produce.

Health Gate
8/F, Hung Tak Bldg., 106 -108 Des Voeux Road, Central
Telephone: 2545 2286
Health Gate has a wide range of frozen organic vegetables and fruits from the United States and soya beans that are not genetically modified.

Cooking Utensil Shops:

CRC Department Stores
92-104 Queen's Road Central
Telephone: 2524 1051 (there are several in Hong Kong)
Good for utensils, some food items and Chinese-cooking equipment, such as rice cookers.

King Tat Hong Porcelain Co
126-128 Queen's Road East, Wanchai
Telephone: 2528 5789
Great source of white plates of every dimension, cake tins and glasses.

Panhandler
343 Prince's Building, Central
Telephone: 2523 1672
Good hunting ground for high-end cake tins, ramekin dishes and cake decorating equipment.

Caterers:

Bayou Catering
Telephone: 2526 2118
Bayou serves New Orleans-style food for every occasion.

Divine Catering
Telephone: 2563 8620
This company has the ability to cater for all events and venues large and small.

Eurest Catering Services
Telephone: 2873 1811
Eurest will cater for large and small events with more than 100 menus to choose from; they can even arrange Chinese dancers and magicians.

Liz Seaton
Telephone: 9331 3024
Liz offers a wide variety of international menus for cocktail, dinner and junk parties.

Oscar's Catering
Telephone: 9301 1145
Oscar's menu is similar to its restaurant food: modern Australian cuisine.

Victoria Thomson
Telephone: 9750 1088
Victoria offers tailor-made menus for cocktail and dinner parties.

Who We Are

Nell Nelson:

Nell Nelson has worked as a food and travel journalist in Hong Kong for seven years. She writes a weekly food column for the *South China Morning Post* and food and travel articles for other publications. She was editor of *Asian Home Gourmet* for 2 years and contributes to *Hong Kong Tatler Best Restaurant Guide*.

Born and educated in Scotland, she worked in London for 5 years as an advertising copywriter. London was where she first started writing about food; she wrote the Afro-Caribbean section of the *TimeOut Eating Guide* as a result of attending Afro-Caribbean cooking classes. Nelson is an enthusiastic, resourceful cook. As a chalet girl in France, she learnt to produce Cordon Bleu 3-course meals for 15 people everyday, on a budget, on top of a mountain and on 1 leg after a skiing accident meant a leg in plaster.

She has an Honours Degree in English Literature from St Andrews University, a Diploma in Advertising Copywriting from Watford College of Art and a Certificate of Completion of the Chinese Dim Sum course from the YWCA, Hong Kong.

A. Chester Ong:

Even the most humble baked bean can look glamorous through his lens. Ong is passionate about food, jazz and travel. He was educated in Manila, where he studied to be a vet before he became fascinated with photography. Ong has his own company, Skylight Productions, in Hong Kong. His work has appeared in magazines such as *Elle*, *Elle Decoration*, *Trends*, *Travel and Leisure* and *Asian Home Gourmet*. He and author Nell Nelson put on a 24-hour-round-the-clock-eating in Hong Kong photo exhibition in 1997.

Rachel Brebner:

Full-time artist and all-the-time foodie, Rachel Brebner completed a Music Degree in Conducting before she traded her baton for a paintbrush. She lives in New Zealand, and is surrounded by an enthusiastic family of food fanatics. She spends several months each year at her studio in Hong Kong painting, designing interiors, illustrating books and exhibiting her art.

My Eat Cook Hong Kong

Use these pages to record the recipes you have enjoyed eating and cooking in Hong Kong and beyond.

My Eat Cook Hong Kong

My Eat Cook Hong Kong